Patchwork with Pizzazz

Over 60 quirky quilts and beautiful bags

Lise Bergene

D&C

David and Charles

A DAVID & CHARLES BOOK

Copyright © J.W Cappelens Forlag 2000, 2005
Originally published in Norway as Kreative Lappe Ideer
Vesker og Bager

First published in the UK in 2006 by David & Charles
David & Charles is an F+W Publications Inc. company
4700 East Galbraith Road
Cincinnati, OH 45236

A catalogue record for this book is available from the British Library.

ISBN-13: 978-0-7153-2552-0 paperback
ISBN-10: 0-7153-2552-3 paperback

Printed in Singapore by KHL Printing company ltd.
for David & Charles
Brunel House   Newton Abbot   Devon

Visit our website at www.davidandcharles.co.uk

David & Charles books are available from all good bookshops;
alternatively you can contact our Orderline on 0870 9908222
or write to us at FREEPOST EX2 110, D&C Direct, Newton Abbot,
TQ12 4ZZ (no stamp required UK only); US customers call
800-289-0963 and Canadian customers call 800-840-5220.

Patchwork
with Pizzazz

Contents

Before You Start . . .

Reading the information here will help you to make the exciting projects in this book. You will find general patchwork and quilting advice here, while pages 64–73 describe basic bag-making techniques and assembly.

MEASUREMENTS AND RULERS

I started using cutting equipment quite early on. The rulers on the market at the time had measurements in inches and that is why I have sewn all of my models using inches. I know that many people use metric rulers and have therefore included metric measurements – being aware that these conversions can never be completely accurate. Do consider this before concluding that my instructions are wrong. *Unless otherwise stated, the seam allowance on all measurements (before sewing together) is ¼in (7mm).*

QUILTING RULER

A while ago I bought a set of rulers called Tri-Recs (see Suppliers). These consisted of two different triangles, which can be used in combination and separately to cut triangles and divide rectangles. There are also six different measures on each triangle, which means that blocks can be sewn in six different sizes.

I have used this ruler for several of the blocks in this book, for instance Rhapsody in Blue, Guinea Hens, You Are My Sunshine, Rich Coffee Quilt, Jungle Rumble, Flowers Wall Hanging and Flora

Quilt. In the instructions for each quilt I give you the measurements to use with a Tri-Recs ruler, and there are also templates; that way you can choose whether to use the ruler or the template.

FABRIC

I wash all my fabrics before using them, to rinse out any superfluous colour and additives as the chemicals that are used can cause allergies. Most of the fabrics I use for patchwork are cotton, but it is possible to use other types of fabrics, such as linen, silk, wool and synthetics. Ultimately, you need to consider what your quilt will be used for when choosing the fabric. Will it be a wall-hanging,

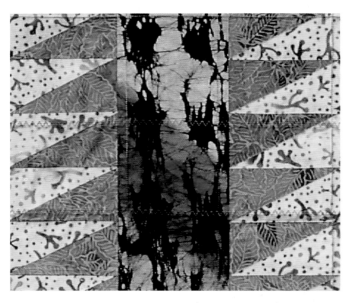

purely for decoration? Or is it intended to warm cold knees? If it requires washing once in a while, make sure to choose a washable fabric.

BATTING

I mostly use pure cotton batting (often called wadding), but there is also wool batting, synthetic batting and cotton/polyester batting available.

APPLIQUÉ WITH DOUBLE-SIDED IRON-ON INTERFACING

You can sew on appliqués with a fusible web such as Bondaweb or Vlisofix either by hand or with your machine, using a range of stitches and thread.
• Trace your chosen design onto the paper side of the interfacing.

- Cut out the design, leaving a little extra space.
- Iron on the interfacing, making sure that the adhesive side is facing the wrong side of the fabric.
- Cut out the design and tear off the backing paper.
- Iron the cut-out design onto the material, with the adhesive side facing the fabric.
- Finally, appliqué the design onto the fabric.

APPLIQUÉ WITH FREEZER PAPER

This technique can be carried out in several ways. I prefer to have the freezer paper on the right side of the appliqué motif, and then fold in the seam allowance with the tip of my needle as I sew.

- Trace the motif to be appliquéd on the matt side of the paper. Cut out the motif along the tracing.
- Iron the freezer paper waxed side down onto the right side of the fabric.
- Cut out the motif with about ³⁄₁₆in (5mm) seam allowance.
- Place the motif where you want it, and tack it on.
- Appliqué with little whipstitches from the right to the left (or *vice versa* if left-handed). Use your needle to fold in the seam allowance as you sew, while holding the seam allowance down with your left thumb (right thumb if left-handed).
- Now you can easily tear off the freezer paper, and no cutting is needed.

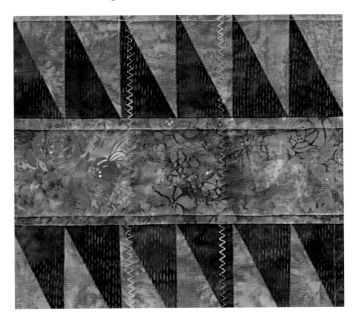

QUILTING

It is possible to quilt patchwork quilts in a variety of ways. You can quilt by hand, using a frame or without one, using regular quilting stitches or a range of different embroidery stitches. If you are machine quilting, you have a number of choices. You can quilt freehand (by lowering the bottom feed dogs, using a darning foot and moving the fabric yourself) – or quilt with a straight seam or other decorative seams, using an upper feed dog. It is probably machine quilting I enjoy the most, because I feel it allows for the most creativity. But my main reason for preferring machine quilting is simply that I like it the best!

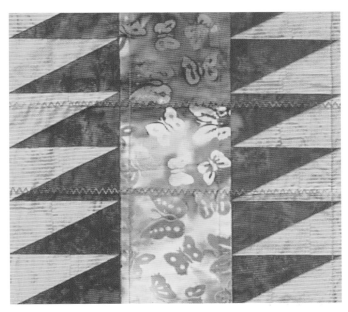

CHOOSING FABRICS AND COLOURS

Many people lack confidence about choosing fabrics. What is right and wrong, and would my quilt look just as good in red as in orange? Can I combine the two? Many would like to know more about colours, but find that it gets too complicated.

Most of us know the Log Cabin technique, where one side is dark and the other light, and the colours themselves are not quite so important. This idea can easily be transferred to other blocks.

My advice is mix the colours that you feel look good together, but include both light and dark colours in your quilt. That, I believe, is important for a successful result.

For some of the models I say that one can use medium colours as well as light and dark ones. You will also see that I use the word shade to mean the degree of light in a fabric, the brightness contrast. If you only use fabrics of the same shade, your quilt will look flat and boring.

So, next time you go shopping, you should also get some boring light fabrics and some dark dreary ones. You will need them for some of the projects in this book.

Picnic Blanket and Bag

This colourful picnic blanket has a handy dual function, doubling as a useful bag.

Finished size of blanket:
33½ x 60½in (85 x 153.7cm)
One block: 9 x 9in (23 x 23cm)

Stitch as follows for the blanket:

- To make one star block, start by cutting two light and two dark squares, each 4 x 4in (10 x 10cm).
- Iron them right sides together, light fabric against dark, and then trace the diagonal on the lightest fabric.
- Follow the instructions for the star block on page 34 from point 3 to point 5.
- Trim the pieces to 3½in x 3½in (9 x 9cm).
- For one star you will also need to cut out four squares each 3½in x 3½in (9 x 9cm) in the fabric for the background and one square of the same size for the middle of the star.

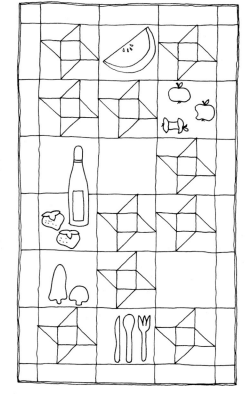

- Sew the star into one block.
- To make up the blanket, make ten different star blocks.
- Cut out nine 9½ x 9½in (24 x 24cm) squares. Some of these can have a large pattern and will need no appliqué. Others should be used as a background for an appliqué (refer to pages 126/127 for all the patterns).
- Sew the blanket together as on the diagram (right).
- Now frame the blanket with a 3½in (9cm) border. This can be cut to the same length as the blocks, i.e. 9½in (24cm). Each corner has a square 3½in x 3½in (9 x 9cm).
- Appliqué the motifs in place. I would use the machine, since a picnic blanket should be sturdy enough to wash.
- Quilt the blanket – preferably on the machine.
- Sew on the binding with the machine from the right side. Don't finish the binding on the back just yet.

Folded up, the blanket has become a bag.

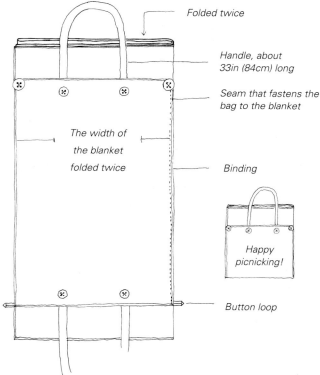

Folded twice

Handle, about 33in (84cm) long

Seam that fastens the bag to the blanket

The width of the blanket folded twice

Binding

Happy picnicking!

Button loop

Stitch as follows for the bag:

- Quilt a piece of fabric with batting and lining, measuring the length of the blanket folded double twice, minus 2¾in (7cm) on either side. This will be the actual bag.
- Sew a binding on three sides of the bag – one long and two short sides.
- Place the bag on the back of the blanket and include two button loops (see diagram, left). These can be made of rope or string.
- Sew the long side of the bag without a binding onto the bound edge and the blanket, and the bag's opposite long side through the blanket.

The bag, attached to the back of the blanket in this way, will make a nice pillow when the blanket is unfolded, so do attach the bag at the end of the blanket.
- Now finish the binding by hand on the back of the blanket, stitching it down neatly.
- Make handles that are 1½in (3.8cm) wide and 33in (84cm) long in double fabric with batting.
- Sew on the handles so that they are sandwiched between the bag and the blanket.
- Make buttonholes on the bag, two at either end by the handles. Sew buttons on the handles and one for each loop to finish.

Strawberries and Cream

My appetite for fabrics is fairly big and my storeroom is well supplied with all kinds of fabric, so I had no trouble finding the right ones for this project. I picked out some strawberry-coloured fabrics from my shelves, and a bag of remnants provided fabrics for the little squares in the block. The fabrics for the squares in between the blocks were supposed to look a bit old-fashioned, and be a lighter shade than strawberry. The quilt has been made in sections for easier quilting on a machine.

Finished size of quilt:
46¾ x 87½in (118.7 x 222.2cm)
One block: 5¾ x 5¾in
(14.5 x 14.5cm)

For one block you will need:
A: 2½ x 2½in (6.4 x 6.4cm), two pieces.
B: 1½ x 1½in (3.8 x 3.8cm), four pieces in a dark and four in a light fabric.
C: 4 x 4in (10 x 10cm), two pieces in a red fabric, cut them diagonally once so that you get four triangles. This gives a size that enables you to trim the block when you have finished sewing it to 6¼ x 6¼in (16 x 16cm).

Stitch as follows:
• Follow the diagram above and sew together the block. For the whole quilt you will need a total of 60 blocks.

  • Cut out the large squares that will go in between the blocks and correspond to the size of the blocks – 6¼ x 6¼in (16 x 16cm).

  • Sew the quilt together with blocks and squares placed alternately in the first row. In the next row the blocks and squares should also alternate, but so that blocks and squares now alternate across both rows and columns, block on top of square, square on top of block, and so on.

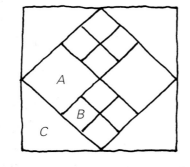

• This quilt is fairly big and so the thought of quilting it on my own sewing machine wasn't very tempting. One alternative is, of course, to quilt by hand. Another is to have the job done professionally – look in the quilting magazines for addresses. My solution was to sew and quilt the design in several pieces. I divided it into one centre piece and two at each end, giving five altogether. This also gave me the opportunity to use different fabrics for the back piece.

• The separate quilt pieces were quilted on my machine with a variety of stitches and with the quilting worked in different directions. The centre piece was worked in a diagonal grid, two were worked with horizontal and vertical lines and were placed on opposite sides of the centre piece. The last two were worked with straight stitches and three-stitch zigzag horizontally and vertically, but the seams were made so that they didn't fit exactly with the quilting lines of the other pieces.

- All the quilt pieces were trimmed. At this point I also checked that the measurements were correct and corresponded to each other, so that the seams would all join up when I sewed the quilt together.
- At the same time as the quilt pieces were sewn together, a strip was included to cover the seam allowance.
- Cut the strip 2in (5cm) wide and iron it double, wrong sides together.
- Measure the seam to be joined and make the strip the same length.
- Place the quilt pieces to be joined up with their right sides together, and put the strip edge to edge with the quilt. The raw edges of the strip should be edge to edge with the raw edges of the quilt pieces. If the strip is a bit too long, just cut off the excess.
- Stitch the shortest seams first.
- Press the strip so that it fully covers the seam allowance and everything is completely flat.

- Sew the strip down by hand.
- Take the next quilt piece (here the centre piece) and sew it onto the two pieces that have been joined up already.
- Finally, sew on the binding, and there you are. Your quilt is finished without the usual struggle to quilt big areas.

This is the back of the quilt.

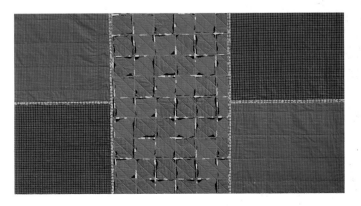

Rhapsody in Blue

I had intended to make this quilt in soft pastels and had got out all my light fabrics ready for use. Sweet, light fabrics from Liberty's of London that I bought many years ago and that were never used – the colours were simply too soft – could now be put to good use. All the light colours have been used, but I have also picked some dark and medium shades in blue, lilac, peacock blue and fairly dark cerise. It didn't turn out all pastels this time either, but I am very pleased with it.

Finished size of quilt:
56 x 89in (142.2 x 226cm)
One block: 8 x 12in (20.3 x 30.5cm)

Stitch as follows:

- Make up the two triangular templates shown in red on page 129 (T4 and 4) in plastic or use a Tri-Recs ruler for a template, cutting line 4½in (11.5cm). These will correspond to shapes T4 and 4 in the diagram, right.
- For one block you need four light blue/lilac of template T4, four dark blue/lilac of template 4 and four dark blue/lilac of the mirror image of template 4. You can also put the fabrics with wrong sides together when you cut them, to get the mirror image effect. You will also need two squares of 4½ x 4½in (11.5 x 11.5cm) in some of your lightest shades.
- Follow the diagram and sew the block together.
- The quilt consists of four by nine blocks. The blocks are placed in the same direction in rows 1, 3, 5, 7 and 9, and in the opposite direction in rows 2, 4, 6 and 8.
- The border around the quilt comprises 4½ x 4½in (11.5 x

11.5cm) squares of the fabrics used with template 4. These shades should be subdivided into very dark and slightly lighter. Two of the darkest and two of the slightly lighter blocks are sewn together and placed alternately along the long sides, making one column of squares. Along the short sides the squares have been joined up into alternate light and dark over two rows.
- My quilt was quilted professionally in impressive-looking whirls.
- The binding is in a dark cerise, which goes well with the dark pink quilting thread.

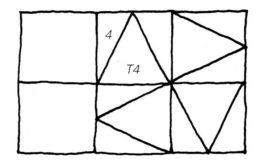

The blocks must face the opposite direction in alternate rows.

Jungle Rumble

Bali fabrics have always been fascinating to me with their wonderful patterns and colours. However, many of them are so beautiful that I can hardly bring myself to cut into them. That's why I was so pleased when this block saw the light of day – at last I had a block which suited all my wonderful Bali fabrics! The loveliest ones were used for the big rectangles, while those that are a little more unobtrusive, dark or fine-patterned, have gone into the triangles.

Finished size of quilt:
48½ x 72½in (123 x 184cm)
One block: 12 x 12in (30.5 x 30.5cm)

Stitch as follows:

- Make the right-angled triangle template on page 129 (number 4, shown in red) in plastic or use a Tri-Recs ruler as a template, cutting line 4½in (11.5cm).
- For one block you need twelve light and twelve dark pieces cut from template 4. If you are cutting several layers at a time, make sure all the fabrics face the right way up so that no triangles turn out facing the wrong way.
- Sew together the light and dark triangles, twelve in all. These must then be sewn onto either side of the rectangle, which must be cut 12½ x 4½in (31.7 x 11.5cm).
- The quilt has four by six blocks placed facing in alternate directions.
- Cotton batting and silk thread were used for the quilting – by machine with straight seams and three-stitch zigzag in horizontal and vertical lines.
- A black fabric with little green/blue lines was used for the binding.

Rich Coffee Quilt

Limiting oneself is a challenge, particularly in the use of fabrics. For this quilt I have only used fabrics designed by Kaffe Fassett and that was a challenge, but at the same time it was great to work with fabrics that were so different. I find this type of work incredibly stimulating!

Finished size: *48½ x 71in (123 x 180.3cm)*

Stitch as follows:

- Make the equilateral triangle template on page 129 (number T6, shown in black) in plastic or use a Tri-Recs ruler as a template, cutting line 6½in (16.5cm).
- Cut out 80 pieces using template T6 in light fabrics (I have used flowery/dotted designs by Kaffe Fassett for my light ones).
- Cut out 72 pieces using template T6 in dark fabrics (I have used striped designs by Kaffe Fassett for my dark ones).
- In the same striped fabrics, cut out 16 pieces using template 6.
- Sew them together with light and dark ones alternating, so that you get four light diamond shapes on the short side of the quilt and ten on the long side.
- At each short end you should use the striped pieces cut using template 6 on page 129.
- One of the very nicest fabrics (dotted black) has been used as a border on the short sides. This strip is cut to 5½in (14cm) along the entire width of the quilt.
- This quilt has been machine quilted along each seam with an embroidery stitch.
- The binding is in the same fabric as that used for the border on the short sides.

Summer Flowers

This is an invitation to all fabric lovers to bring you flowers, blocks and, hopefully, lots of inspiration. I will give you the basic information you need and leave you to work the rest out for yourself.

The appliqué patterns for the pot, flowers and leaves are on page 128. The centre piece measures 19 x 21in (48.3 x 53.3cm) and the width of the strips bordering the centre piece is 1½in (3.8cm). Instructions for making the bottom left corner block are on page 10.

Finished size:
28½ x 32½in (72.4 x 82.5cm)

Flowers Wall Hanging

This wall hanging was begun at a school in Skirringsal in Sandefjord in 1999. Every year in August my sewing group organizes a weekend course at this school. That year each participant was asked to cut a flower and a leaf out of freezer paper for me. This they did, and I have included them all in this bouquet. As these flowers were personal gifts to me, I don't want to pass on the patterns to others. But I am happy to pass on the idea!

Finished size:
24 x 31in (61 x 79cm)

Cut out the flowers and anything else you fancy, for instance letters or numbers, in freezer paper (see page 7). Use these as patterns and appliqué them on, either by hand or by machine. You will soon discover what fun it is to make your own motifs – and it's easy, too!

The hanging has a background of dark fabrics, and I have used soft pastels as a contrast in the flowers and vase. I made the '2000' and 'LB' patterns myself: these shapes have somewhat

darker colours than the flowers. I have embroidered stamens in the flower centres using embroidery thread.

The bottom edge of the wall hanging consists of alternating light and dark triangles. Use template 3 on page 129 or cutting line 3½in (9cm) on a Tri-Recs ruler.

I have machine-quilted this wall hanging freehand, using shiny embroidery thread.

Linen Tablecloth

This tablecloth is made out of one large piece of linen. This was washed and ironed and the blocks were appliquéd on with silk ribbon. You can choose the size of this cloth yourself, since the size of the linen determines the size of the tablecloth.

Finished size:
55 x 73in (140 x 185cm)
One block: 6 x 6in (15.2 x 15.2cm)

Stitch as follows:
- Make templates T6 and 6 on page 129 (shown in black) in plastic or use a Tri-Recs ruler as a template, cutting line 6½in (16.5cm).
- For each block you will need one piece of light fabric in the size of template T6, one of template 6 and one of template 6 inverted in a dark fabric.
- Sew the block following the small diagram.
- The tablecloth has 48 blocks – 24 for the centre piece and 12 along each side. The linen was first washed and ironed. The blocks were then made and sewn together into a 24-block centre piece, 2 blocks wide and 12 blocks long. See the large diagram for the direction and the positioning of the blocks.
- The side row blocks were sewn together with 12 blocks in each row. See diagram for positioning.
- The centre piece was appliquéd onto the linen using a silk ribbon about ⅜in (10mm) wide, on both sides of the centre piece. Sew the ribbon on with a straight machine stitch along both the outer edges.
- The side rows were also appliquéd on the linen with silk ribbon, but only on one side. The other side was included in the binding.
- I wasn't sure that this tablecloth needed any quilting, but since I found a thin, synthetic batting without too much volume, I ended up machine quilting it in simple lines. The lines follow the seams in the blocks, creating diagonal lines.
- The binding for the tablecloth is purple.

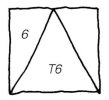

Block for linen tablecloth

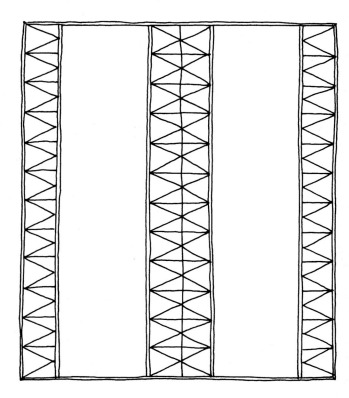

Silk and Linen Runner

Combining linen and silk creates a lovely contrast in terms of both structure and lustre. The centre piece of this runner is linen, while the appliquéd pieces are silk. There is a good mixture of colours, with dark shades of lilac, blue, purple and green. I based my lighter colours on the colour of the linen which is a greenish yellow. I also included a bit of yellow, light ochre and one fabric that comes close to turquoise.

Finished size:
17½ x 48½in (44.5 x 123.2cm)
One edge block: 2 x 4in (5 x 10cm)

Stitch as follows for the edge block:

This procedure will give you four edge blocks.
- **X:** Cut out one square of 5¼ x 5¼in (13.3 x 13.3cm).
- **Y:** Cut out four squares of 2⅞ x 2⅞in (7.3 x 7.3cm).
- Trace diagonal lines on the wrong side of all Y squares.
- Place two Y squares on top of an X square, right sides together, so that the traced diagonals meet.

- Sew along both sides of the diagonal with a ¼in (7mm) seam allowance, as shown in A. Cut along the diagonal line.
- Press the little triangles away from the big one (B).
- Place a Y square on each of these pieces, right sides together, so the diagonal goes from the corner to the centre.
- Sew along both sides of the diagonal leaving a seam allowance of ¼in (7mm). Cut along the diagonal line (C).
- Press the little triangles away from the big one (D).

Stitch as follows for the runner:

Cut referring to the diagram:
- **A:** 11½ x 40½in (29.2 x 103cm) for the centre piece in linen.
- **B:** 4½ x 11½in (11.5 x 29.2cm) the short side border.
- **C:** 4½ x 13½in (11.5 x 34.2cm) the short side border.
- **D:** Two pieces of 2½ x 4½in (6.4 x 11.5cm) for two corners.
- **E:** Make 33 edge blocks – see separate instructions.
- Now sew the decorations on the linen centre piece. Use black silk thread and sew diagonal lines. There is no

need to trace them in advance, as they are meant to be a little wavy and irregular. I quilted in these lines later on.
- Sew the pieces together, following the diagram below.
- Appliqué on flowers and leaves (templates on page 128) with double-sided iron-on interfacing (see page 6), or whatever appliqué technique you prefer.
- Quilt the runner freehand by following the seams on the centre piece. Use wavy lines with an extra swirl here and there. Begin and finish the quilting at the edge.
- The binding used here is made from a very dark fabric.

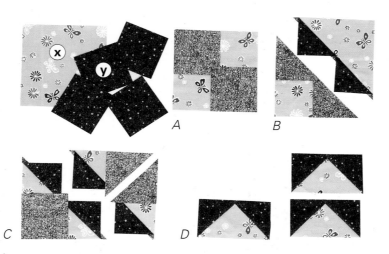

22

Flora Quilt

For this quilt I have used colours such as orange, pink, dark lilac and dark red. The border is a black fabric with green and blue checks. I have repeated those colours in lighter shades in the appliqué.

Finished size:
31½ x 34½in (80 x 87.6cm)
One block: 3 x 3in (7.6 x 7.6cm)

Stitch the quilt as follows:

- Make templates T3 and 3 on page 129 (shown in purple) in plastic or use a Tri-Recs ruler as a template, cutting line 3½in (9cm).
- All the fabrics need to be cut out with all the templates.
- For one block you need one piece from template T3, one from template 3 and one from template 3 inverted. Alternate dark and light colours in the same position in the blocks.
- Sew them together following the block diagram.
- The quilt has 56 blocks, eight high by seven wide for the centre piece.
- Cut out the border fabric 5½in (14cm) wide.
- The corner squares measure 5½ x 5½in (14 x 14cm).
- Sew the quilt together and appliqué stalks and flowers on the border – the instructions follow.
- This quilt is machine quilted in circles with silk thread.
- I used a multicoloured fabric for the binding.

Stitch the stalks and flowers as follows:

- The stalks are all made of bias binding. Cut out 1¼in (3.2cm) wide fabric strips diagonally on the bias and iron them double, wrong sides together.
- Place them on the quilt in soft wavy lines. This will be simple because the fabric has been cut on the bias.
- Sew them on the border by hand, with little tacking stitches and a few backstitches along the middle of the double bias binding.
- Cut the raw edges down to half and iron the binding slightly across so that it covers the raw edges.
- Sew the bias binding down by hand in the fold, using tiny whipstitches.
- Appliqué the flowers, leaves and buds on by hand using the freezer paper technique (see page 7).

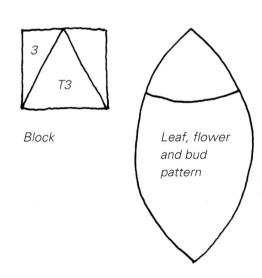

Block

Leaf, flower and bud pattern

Pretty Pouches

Medium large pouch

Stitch as follows for a large pouch:

- You will need about 12 x 31½in (30.5 x 80cm) of linen, with the batting and lining a little bigger than the linen.
- If you are going to decorate the pouch (see photo overleaf), this can be done now or when you've quilted your work.
- Quilt the bag any way you like, then trim.
- Decorate your pouch now if you haven't done so already (templates on page 131).
- Place the pouch piece double, wrong sides together, and sew the side seams with a seam allowance of ³⁄₁₆in (5mm).
- Turn the bag inside out so that its right sides are together and sew the side seams, this time with a seam allowance of ⅜in (10mm). Make sure the last set of seams encloses the previous seam allowances. This seam is called a French seam.
- Now fold in to make a corner at the bottom end of each side seam, so that the bottom corners point towards the middle of the bottom, and sew a seam across the corner 1¼in (3cm) in from the tip. In other words, a false bottom.
- Cut a strip of 1½in (4cm) that reaches around the opening of the bag plus about 1¾in (4.5cm).
- Sew on the strip from the wrong side of the pouch.
- Fold in the seam allowance and sew it on with a machine seam from the right side.
- Create two casings from two fabric strips measuring 2 x 8in (5 x 20.3cm).
- Seal the long sides of the casings with a zigzag seam.
- Fold, iron, and sew a seam in each short side.
- Fold in and iron ⅜in (10mm) on all long sides.
- Attach the casings with a seam 2in (5cm) from the top edge of the pouch.
- Insert two drawstrings, 28in (70cm) long, from each side and all the way round.
- Tie the drawstrings together with a knot. Pull the drawstrings to close the pouch.

Pouches are useful for lots of things – maybe your sewing things or other necessities we need to carry around from time to time. You can choose your own size or follow my measurements. I will also suggest some decoration ideas, but you can, of course, decorate it however you like. I will give you measurements for three different sizes and tell you how to sew them. See page 131 for the appliqué patterns.

Finished measurements (more or less, depending on your seam allowance):
Large pouch: 10½ x 15in (26.7 x 38cm)
Medium pouch: 6¾ x 9in (17 x 23cm)
Small pouch: 6 x 8in (15.2 x 20.3cm)

Stitch as follows for a medium pouch:

- My bag is made of eight rectangles 4 x 5in (10 x 12.7cm), two across and four down.
- The batting and lining should be slightly bigger than the patchwork for the outside.
- Quilt the piece with an embroidery seam or straight seam by machine.
- Trim the piece.
- Appliqué on the heart (template on page 133) with a close zigzag seam.
- From here on, follow the instructions for the big pouch, with one exception: sew the side seams with wrong sides together and seal the raw edges with a three-stitch zigzag. Don't do a French seam, as it will be too thick for this size pouch.
- Fold the bottom corners and sew them ¾in (2cm) from the tip.
- Cut the casings 2 x 5½in (5 x 14cm) and sew them on 1in (2.5cm) from the top edge.
- The drawstrings are 17in (43cm) long.

Stitch as follows for a small pouch:

- Cut up 40 squares of 2 x 2in (5 x 5cm), and sew them together four across and ten down.
- Quilt the piece with the batting and lining and then trim the piece.
- Sew the side seams with wrong sides together and seal the raw edges with a three-stitch zigzag.
- Fold the bottom corners and sew them ¾in (2cm) from the tip.
- Then follow the instructions for the large pouch.
- Cut the casings 1½ x 5½in (3.8 x 14cm) and sew them on 1in (2.5cm) from the top edge.
- The drawstrings are 15in (38cm) long.

Small pouch

Guinea Hens

This guinea hen wall hanging is great fun to make. Use the appliqué patterns on page 131.

Finished size of wall hanging:
11¾ x 48¾in (30 x 124cm)
Triangle block: 3 x 3in (7.6 x 7.6cm)
Egg block: 2¾ x 4½in (7 x 11.5mm)
Egg flower block: 2¾ x 6in (7 x 15.2cm)

Stitch as follows:

- Cut out background fabrics for the hens. The backgrounds for the top and bottom hens measure 8¾ x 12½in (22.2 x 31.75cm) and the middle one measures 8¾ x 11in (22.2 x 28cm).
- Copy the hens on freezer paper (see page 7), and appliqué them on with beak, tail and comb.
- Sew 18 triangle blocks – use the same colourways and technique as on the Flora Quilt on page 24.
- Make three egg blocks by cutting out three fabric pieces of 3¼ x 5in (8.2 x 12.7cm) and appliqué on three eggs.
- Make three egg flower blocks: sew together three pieces of fabric each 3¼ x 6½in (8.2 x 16.5cm) and then appliqué three flowers with stems and put them a little on top of each other.
- The first hen will be accompanied by four triangle blocks on the right side. Sew them together.
- The second hen will have three egg blocks above her and five triangle blocks along the left side.
- The third hen has a bigger fence between herself and her neighbour. Sew one row of three egg flower blocks with two triangle blocks at the right side. Stitch four triangle blocks on the left of the hen then join the fence and hen sections.
- The bottom line is made up of three triangle blocks plus one piece of fabric to match them.
- This piece has been spot-quilted in the shape of small circles and some straight seams on the triangle blocks. I did this on the machine using embroidery thread.
- To help them see better, the hens have been given button eyes.
- I finished my hen piece with a binding in multicoloured stripes.

Left *Large pouch (instructions on page 26)*

You Are My Sunshine

There is normally a pencil and some paper on my worktop when I'm cooking, so that I can draw and doodle design ideas. One of the results is the design you see here. See page 132 for all the appliqué patterns.

Finished size:
18 x 24½in (45.7 x 62.2cm)

Stitch as follows:

- Cut out the pieces following the measurements on the diagram and sew them together. The triangle blocks are the same as in the Flora Quilt on page 24.
- Copy the appliqué patterns with double-sided iron-on interfacing (see page 6) and sew them on with a close zigzag or other appliqué stitches. Check your machine, as it may have several good appliqué stitches to choose from.
- I thought freehand machine quilting suited this project well. I have also written, freehand, the words 'You are my sunshine' in Norwegian as part of the quilting.
- A few buttons have been added as a decoration, and the piece has been given a dark binding.

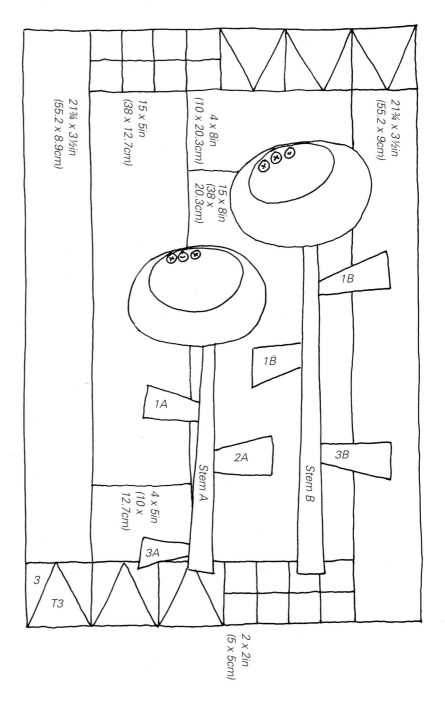

21¾ x 3½in (55.2 x 8.9cm)

15 x 5in (38 x 12.7cm)

4 x 8in (10 x 20.3cm)

21¾ x 3½in (55.2 x 9cm)

15 x 8in (38 x 20.3cm)

1B

1B

1A

2A

3B

Stem A

Stem B

4 x 5in (10 x 12.7cm)

3A

3

T3

2 x 2in (5 x 5cm)

Building Houses

Sometimes I take ages picking fabrics for a project, and that was certainly true in this case. One fabric after the other was taken out from its shelf, but nothing seemed to be just right. Finally, I decided that the sky should be as dark as the night. Then I decided what colour each house façade should have, and then I chose the colours for windows, doors and roofs.

All the time I had to bear in mind the light/ dark contrast. Houses and roofs must be visible against the dark sky, and so I had to use lighter colours. Had I decided on a light- coloured sky, the houses would have had to be darker. I picked out several checked fabrics. These often have more colours and contrasts than fabrics with smaller patterns, so they more easily mix with and reflect other fabrics.

My house building project finally took off in a big way – I found it hard to stop! I made place mats, a row of houses, a pouch and a quilt for Mona. But just between you and me, I still have a few house blocks in store!

House I

Finished size: *5¼ x 11¼in (13.3 x 28.5cm)*

For one block:
A: 5¾ x 2in (14.6 x 5cm), one piece for background;
B: 1¾ x 1¾in (4.4 x 4.4cm), two pieces for background, quick corners;
C: 5¾ x 2¾in (14.6 x 7cm), one piece for roof;
D: 5¾ x 2in (14.6 x 5cm), two pieces for house;
E: 2 x 1¼in (5 x 3.2cm), four pieces for house;
F: 2 x 1¼in (5 x 3.2cm), three pieces for windows;
G: 3½ x 2¾in (8.9 x 7cm), one piece for house;

House 1

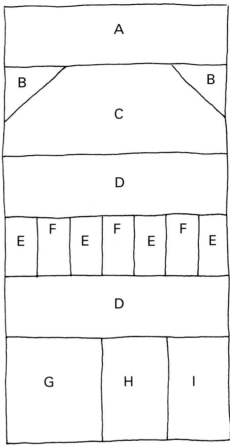

H: 3½ x 2in (8.9 x 5cm), one piece for door;
I: 3½ x 2in (8.9 x 5cm), one piece for house.

House 2

Finished size: *5 x 11¼in (12.7 x 28.5cm)*

For one block:
A: 5½ x 5in (14 x 12.7cm), one piece
  for background;
B: 2 x 2in (5 x 5cm) two pieces for
  background, quick corners;
C: 5½ x 2in (14 x 5cm), one piece for roof;
D: 5½ x 1½in (14 x 3.8cm) two pieces for house;
E: 1½ x 1½in (3.8 x 3.8cm), three pieces
  for house;
F: 1½ x 1½in (3.8 x 3.8cm), two pieces
  for windows;
G: 2¾ x 1½in (7 x 3.8cm) one piece for house;
H: 2¾ x 2¾in (7 x 7cm), one piece for door;
I: 2¾ x 2¼in (7 x 5.7cm), one piece for house.

House 3

Finished size: *4½ x 11¼in (10.8 x 28.5cm)*

For one block:
J: 5 x 3½in (12.7 x 8.9cm), one piece
  for background;
K: 5 x 2¾in (12.7 x 7cm), one piece for roof;
L: 2 x 6½in (5 x 16.5cm), two pieces for house;
M: 2 x 1½in (5 x 3.8cm), three pieces for house;
N: 2 x 2in (5 x 5cm), two pieces for window.

Quick corners; stitch as follows:

• Put square X (part B on houses 1 and 2) on the
  roof fabric and sew the diagonal (see below).
• Cut off the outside corner of the square with the
  seam allowance, leaving the roof fabric.
• Iron the remaining triangle towards the corner.

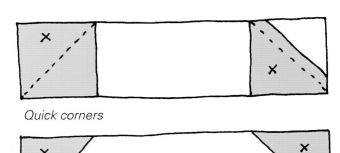

Quick corners

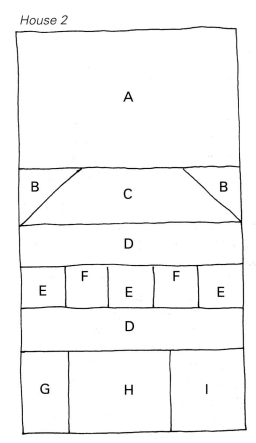

House 2

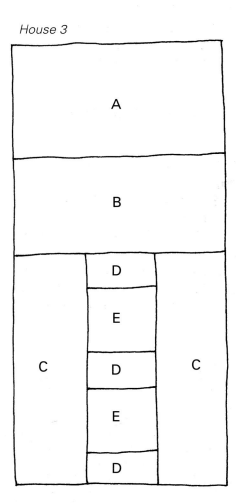

House 3

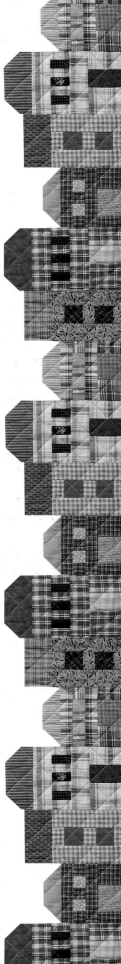

Star Block
Finished size: *3 x 3in (7.6 x 7.6cm)*

- Cut two light squares for a star and two background squares. Each should be 2 x 2in (5 x 5cm).
- Iron them right sides together, light against dark (star fabric against background fabric) and trace the diagonal with a pencil on the lighter fabric.
- Sew along both sides of the diagonal line with a seam allowance of ¼in (7mm).
- Iron lightly and cut along the traced diagonal line.
- Press the triangles open placing the seam allowance against the darker fabric.
- Trim the squares to 1½ x 1½in (3.8 x 3.8cm).
- To make one star you will also need four squares of 1½ x 1½in (3.8 x 3.8cm) in background fabric, and one square the same size in star fabric for the middle of the star.
- The block should measure 3½ x 3½in (9 x 9cm) before it is sewn together.

Bow Tie Block
Finished block size:
6 x 6in (15.2 x 15.2cm)

- Cut two light and two dark squares each 4 x 4in (10 x 10cm).
- Iron them right sides together, light against dark, and trace the diagonal with a pencil on the lighter fabric.
- Follow the procedure for the star block from point 3 to 5, above.
- Trim the squares to 3½ x 3½in (9 x 9cm).
- Sew them together as in the drawing above.
- The block should measure 6½ x 6½in (16.5 x 16.5cm) before it is sewn together.

Drawstring Bag

Stitch as follows:
- Sew two of house 1, one of house 2 and two of house 3.
- Make an extra sky for each house with a 2½in (6.3cm) fabric strip the width of the house.
- Sew them into a row.
- Quilt with batting and lining in a diagonal grid.
- Trim the whole piece to 13¾ x 25in (35 x 63.5cm), but leave about ¾in (2cm) of the lining on one of the short sides. This will be folded over the raw edges in the seam allowance once the seam has been stitched.
- Sew down the hem in the lining by hand.
- Make two casings 2½ x 12in (6.3 x 30.5cm). Fold in about ½in (1.2cm) twice on the short side, and once on the long sides.
- Attach the casings about 1½in (3.8cm) from the top edge of the bag.
- Cover the top edge with a strip that is machine-sewn on from the right side. Fold it over and fasten on the wrong side with hand stitches.
- To make the bottom of the bag, quilt a fabric with lining and batting to measure about 8 x 10in (20.3 x 25.4cm). Cut it out using the oval bag bottom template on page 130.
- Sew the bottom on the bag by putting inside against inside while including bias binding. The bias binding must be folded over the raw edges and sewn down by hand.
- Insert 28in (71cm) long drawstrings from each side and right around, and tie them together with a knot.
- Appliqué on a few stars here and there with blanket stitches by hand (patterns on page 130).

Table Mats
Finished size:
11¾ x 15¼in
(30 x 39cm)

Why not hang your
place mats on the
wall? The place mats
are made from three
house blocks and
machine quilted in a
diagonal grid.

Row of Houses

This wall hanging was such fun to do and would make a great focal point in any room.

Finished size:
36 x 19½in (91.5 x 49.5cm)

Stitch as follows:

- Pick out two of each of the three house block types, but don't sew them together yet.
- Sew six star blocks – use red, orange, yellow and yellowish green fabrics for the stars.
- Lay out the house blocks and put the star blocks above the sky – the stars will form the beginning of a border that will circle the quilt.
- Cut short strips 3½in (9cm) wide in a few dark fabrics. Cut them to the width of the house blocks and put them where there are no stars.
- Fill in the open space by the star blocks by fastening a strip to the star block. Measure the house block it is to stand above and cut the star block to fit.
- You will need a border on either side of the row of houses: 3½ x 11¼in (9 x 28.5cm).
- Cut a rectangle for each of the bottom corners, 3½ x 5in (9 x 12.7cm).
- There is a piece of dark green fabric under each house, as wide as each house and 5in (12.7cm) high.
- Lay out all the pieces and begin sewing together by sewing each part of the border, top as well as bottom, onto the house block. Add the borders on the short sides.
- Appliqué flowers and leaves on the border using the hen's comb and tail patterns on page 131 with the interfacing method on page 6.
- Quilt with straight machine seams. My seams are wavy on the border to give life and movement.
- The binding is a purple fabric.

For Mona

This brightly coloured quilt is perfect for a child's room.

Finished size: *55½ x 84in (141 x 213cm)*

Stitch as follows:

- Make 48 bow tie blocks from page 34. Sew them into a centre piece four blocks wide and 12 long.
- Make 11 blocks of house 1, ten blocks of house 2 and ten blocks of house 3 (pages 32–33).
- Join up the houses in this order: 1-2-3-1-2-3-1-2-3-1-2-3-1-2-3-1-2-3-1 for one row of houses and 1-2-3-1-2-3-1-2-3-1-2-3-1-2-3 for the other.
- Sew two strips of different fabrics that are as dark as the sky in the house blocks. These strips should be 5in (12.7cm) high. They consist of as many cut-up pieces as there are houses in each row. *Note: each house has its own width.*
- Cut each of the strips in two, making them 2½in (6.3cm) high. Each length equals one row of houses.
- Sew these strips on at the top edge and bottom edge of each row of houses and put the rows of houses against the centre piece with the roofs facing the centre.
- Both rows of houses will now be longer than the centre piece. Solve this by sewing each row of houses to the centre piece with one house sticking out on diagonally opposite corners. The seams should not be taken right to the edge, as an extra strip must be sewn on at each short side. So, put the quilt down flat and measure how much the row of houses sticks out. This will be the width of the extra strip. Also measure the width of the quilt, from the house row and to the edge: that will be the length of the extra strip. Cut a strip to this measurement (and include seam allowances).
- Sew on the strips.
- I appliquéd hearts and letters on the broadest strip using a close zigzag.
- I quilted with straight machine seams in horizontal and vertical lines, using silk for my upper thread and cotton for the lower thread.
- The binding is in a dark blue fabric with an almost invisible pattern.

1999

I was very attracted to the idea of using some little blocks I had made already. And why not? Old blocks were retrieved from drawers and cupboards, put next to each other and scrutinized, several times over. The solution was to appliqué the blocks into a bouquet as if they were flowers.

I appliquéd the blocks with coarse cross stitches in silk thread, and did not fold in any seam allowance. I trimmed the edges, of course, to make them look neat and straight. I did the same for the vase. Leaves and stalks have been hand-appliquéd, however, using freezer paper.

I have an inkling you might have a few blocks in your cupboard, so you will only need measurements for the background.

Finished size: *30 x 34½in (76 x 87.6cm)*

Stitch as follows:

- Cut a 20 x 24½in (51 x 62cm) rectangle in neutral fabric to make a good background for your appliqué.
- The border is divided into two strips, 2½in (6.3cm) wide on all four sides, with identical blocks in each corner.
- The corner blocks are sewn over thin card (like English paper piecing), with identical fabrics (see page 130 for the corner block pattern).
- Sew the strips together, and then sew the strips on the centre piece. Finally, sew on the corner blocks by hand.

- Pin the vase a little to the left in the centre piece.
- Appliqué on leaves and stalks by hand with freezer paper (see page 7).
- Now the rest of the blocks and a few little squares can be put in place and all the pieces tacked on before you start the actual appliqué.
- I have worked the appliqué with coarse cross stitches in silk thread.
- The same coarse cross stitches were used for the appliqué of 1999.
- I freehand quilted my work on the machine using a multicoloured silk thread and added a few buttons for added decoration.
- The binding is in a dark pattern and was sewn on right at the end.

For Father

A quilt in brushed cotton fabrics is a wonderful gift for your beloved – just the thing for a quick nap on the sofa! It is both soft and warm on a chilly evening. If you decorate it with big hearts, the thought behind your gift should be very clear.

I was lucky enough to be given some brushed cotton samples. The pieces were about the same width, but had different lengths. To make the most of the samples I cut them all to the same width but left the different lengths. That way, very little fabric was lost.

Finished size:
49½ x 68in (125.7 x 172.7cm)

Stitch as follows:

- Cut up pieces of the same width but with different lengths in brushed cotton fabrics. My pieces are 7½in (19cm) wide, and 3–15½in (7.6–39.4cm) long.
- Sew the pieces together into seven strips that are roughly the same length. None of the seams should match up.
- Cut out some hearts in paper without tracing them in advance. They should all be different and have a naïve look.
- Use the paper hearts as a pattern and appliqué them on, spreading them all over the quilt.
- This quilt is hand quilted with big stitches along the seams and around each heart. I have used red pearl (perlé) cotton, and since this thread is thicker than ordinary quilting thread, I had to do my quilting with an embroidery needle. I have also tied some knots in the pieces where there is no heart.
- The binding is in a red cotton fabric.

Hen Table Mat

I promise you people will sit up and take notice if you lay your table with these table mats. They are quick to make, and if you should be lucky enough to have three triangle squares left over from the bow tie blocks on page 34, all you need is one square in the same fabric as the lightest colour in the triangle squares.

Finished size:
12½ x 15¾in (31.7 x 40cm)

Stitch as follows:

- Sew together three triangle squares and one square of 3½ x 3½in (9 x 9cm), and you've got the tail.
- The body measures 13 x 12½in (33 x 31.7cm) and is sewed on the tail.

- Machine appliqué the beak using interfacing (see page 6).
- Quilt the mat with a few lines and a simple recipe or some nice words.
- Sew on a couple of buttons for eyes and two straight seams for eyebrows.
- Trim the entire hen and finish with a binding.

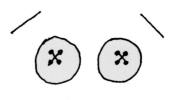
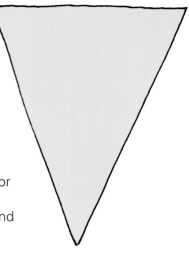

Holmen Farm

During the summer of 1999 I taught at Holmen Farm, which is something of a centre for Norwegian arts and crafts. The teachers and students sleep, eat and attend the courses there from Sunday evening until Friday afternoon. The days are full and intense, with lots of sewing and much good food, so time flies.

This was the first time I taught a course at Holmen Farm, therefore it was a very special occasion. I wanted to make a wall hanging as a reminder of the week, using flowers and leaves from each of the course participants. Using their imagination, everyone cut a flower and a leaf in freezer paper, ironed them on their chosen fabrics, and gave them to me. When I got back home and took them all out, It was fascinating to see how different all the flowers were in shape and colour. But even though they were so different, they had to be gathered into one bouquet. Since I was the teacher, I wanted to be in the hanging, too. See all the hexagons? That's me.

Finished size:
15½ x 22in (39.3 x 56cm)

45

Pincushion

Here's a small and easy pincushion, which you can make in no time.

Start with a small piece of fabric – the procedure is the same, whether you have a fabric in one piece or comprised of many patches.

Stitch as follows:

- The piece you need measures 3½ x 4½in (9 x 11.5cm). If your piece is a patchwork, line it with some other fabric.
- Fold the longest side double, right sides together and sew both the short seams.
- Place the short seams right sides together.
- Sew from the corner about ¾in (2cm), skip about 1¼in (3.2cm) and sew all the way out to the next corner.
- Turn the pincushion the right way out and fill with bird sand.
- Sew up the hole with little whipstitches.
- Sew a button in the centre simultaneously with a button on the underside using embroidery thread. Fasten the thread by tying a knot on the top button.

Bobbins Runner and Mat

I have made this runner and the table mats out of many remnants, so the colours are chosen somewhat at random. However, there's nothing random about the interplay between light and dark fabrics. The bobbins are made in the darkest fabrics I could find, and the backgrounds in lighter fabrics. It was a fun way to use up some of my remnants.

Finished sizes:
Runner 15½ x 39½in (39.3 x 100.3cm)
Mat 12½ x 16¼in (31.7 x 41.3cm)

Finished size of bobbin block:
6 x 6in (15.2 x 15.2cm)

Stitch the bobbin block as follows:

A: Cut out two squares each 4 x 4in (10 x 10cm), a light one for the background and a darker one for the bobbin. Iron them right sides together and follow instructions for the bow tie block on page 34.

B: Cut out two squares of 3½ x 3½in (9 x 9cm). These should have the same light shade or fabric as the lightest triangle in point A.

C: Cut two squares of 2 x 2in (5 x 5cm) in a fabric that goes well with the darkest triangle in point A.

- Now put C on B and sew quick corners as described on page 33.
- Stitch the block as in the diagram.

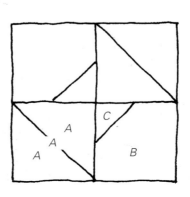

Bobbin block

Stitch the runner as follows:

- Take 12 bobbin blocks and sew them together, two blocks wide by six blocks long.
- Make a 2in (5cm) border around the whole piece.
- Machine quilt the runner with a simple machine embroidery stitch.
- Finally, sew on a binding. Notice how four bobbin blocks form a new block.

Stitch the mat as follows:

- Take two bobbin blocks and sew them together with a piece of fabric that measures 10¼ x 12½in (26 x 31.7cm).
- I machine quilted the table mat with diagonal as well as horizontal lines using a simple machine embroidery stitch.
- The mat has a red binding.

47

I go to the sales, you go to the sales, but my dear friend Ellen Borge does not. She lets others do that job for her, such as for instance Lise Bergene. The lady doesn't always approve of the fabrics I buy for her, and of course she has the right to return them! That way I often end up with more fabrics than intended.

If Ellen should decide to visit the sales one day (which I doubt, since I am still a useful shopping maid!) a new world would open up to her. One can just imagine how she would visit every single quilting shop in Scandinavia that has a sale on – even England would be graced by visits from this keen quilter from Norway.

Finished size of quilt:

31½ x 35½in (80 x 90cm)

A: Bobbin block 6 x 6in (15.2 x 15.2cm)

B: Roof sides: 6 x 6in (15.2 x 15.2cm)

Stitch as follows:

A: Make three bobbin blocks as described on page 46.

B: Roof sides – use the same technique as for the bobbin block, but with different measurements. Cut the squares to 7 x 7in (17.8 x 17.8cm), one light and one dark. Trim the roof sides to 6½ x 6½in (16.5 x 16.5cm). Then follow the diagram below for further cutting and joining.

- Appliqué the seamstress and the letters, using interfacing (see page 6). I have appliquéd with a close zigzag on the machine, using black silk thread. The figure's hair and thin legs have been zigzagged on with cotton yarn. The patterns for the appliqué are on pages 133–136.
- This quilt has also been decorated with some buttons, little fabric pieces and some clothes' labels.
- The quilting was done by machine – some of it freehand, some using the upper feed dogs.
- The binding is sewn on at the end.

B	6½ x 19½in (16.5 x 49.5cm)		B
3½ x 17½in (8.9 x 44.5cm)	3½ x 17½in (8.9 x 44.5cm)	23½ x 19½in (59.7 x 49.5cm)	3½ x 23½in (9 x 59.7cm) 3½ x 23½in (9 x 59.7cm)
A			
A	A	6½ x 19½in (16.5 x 49.5cm)	

48

Play Houses

Are you brave enough to have a go with a knife and ruler, no measurements, but lots of purpose? The houses will be built with a certain amount of control, but there will always be room for your own measurements and estimates.

Finished size of quilt:
*36½ x 48in (92.7 x 122cm)
House block: 14½ x 14½in (36.8 x 36.8cm)
One block with a square on:
6½ x 6½in (16.5 x 16.5cm)*

Stitch as follows for a house block:

- Draw a house on paper, with walls and roof a little askew. It should measure about 6–9 x 8½–11in (15–23 x 21.5–28cm).
- Make a visual estimate by looking at each part to be cut out. Now cut out each part of the house using your eye measure. You can use a ruler to get the lines straight.
- Sew the parts together. To get a straight seam it's best to trim the line before the next bit is sewn on.
- Cut out strips of the background fabric, again by eye.
- Sew on the strips on all sides of the house.
- Trim the blocks to make them properly square or rectangular, i.e. with 90 degree corners.
- Sew on a strip and a border as on

the drawing. The strip should be 1¼ in (3.2cm) wide and the border 3in (7.6cm) wide. Use your ruler for these strips.
- Put a 15 x 15in (38 x 38cm) ruler askew on the block and cut off the surplus fabric.

Stitch as follows for a block with a square on:

- First make a visual estimate of a square that measures 4 x 4in (10 x 10cm).
- Cut out three squares according to this estimate. One square becomes A. Two squares are cut diagonally and become four B triangles.
- Sew all four B triangles on the A square.
- Cut the block so you get straight lines, however the corners shouldn't be exactly 90 degrees.
- Sew on strips with a width of plus/minus 1½in (3.8cm).
- Cut the block to 7 x 7in (17.8 x 17.8cm), but this time *with* 90 degree corners.

- Now follow the picture to sew the quilt together. It has six house blocks that have been combined into two rows, cut up and then combined with a total of seven blocks with a square on.
- Machine quilt the quilt in freehand loops and waves.
- The binding has stripes in many of the same colours as the quilt.

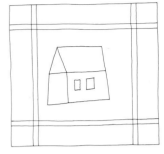

House block before cutting

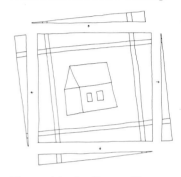

House block after cutting

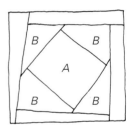

Block with a square on

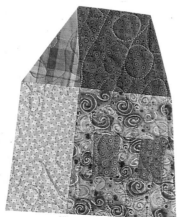

Witches' Celebration

I am a member of a fabric club, and every second month they send me fabric samples. These are big enough to be trimmed and used in patchwork, like here in the Witches' Celebration. To bring out all the colours and nuances of the stripes I have chosen fairly dark fabrics and some totally black ones, for the big and little squares.

Finished size:
45½ x 83½in (115.5 x 212cm)

Stitch as follows:

- Cut out strips of 1½ x 3in (3.8 x 7.6cm) in many different fabrics, or use the samples from your fabric club.
- Sew together five strips into one set – this quilt has a total of 115 sets.
- Cut 50 big dark squares that measure 5½ x 5½in (14 x 14cm). They will be placed five wide by ten high.
- Cut 66 dark squares each 3 x 3in (7.6 x 7.6cm).
- Follow the diagram, right, when you sew the quilt together.

- The quilt has been given a border made up of the darkest fabrics – these measure 3 x 8in (7.6 x 20.3cm). You will have to adjust the border a bit in all four corners, as it will be a little too long.
- My quilt has been stipple quilted with multi-coloured thread that picks up on the colours in the patches. I had this done professionally.
- For the binding I chose a big-patterned fabric that also brings out the colours in the patches.
- The back of the quilt is in brushed cotton, so that it will feel nice and warm on your feet on a chilly evening.

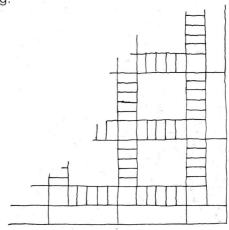

Magically Easy

This is a quilt for decoration only (see picture overleaf). I don't even know if it's washable! But it's a long time since I had so much fun during the sewing process.

The witches have been machine-appliquéd on, with an uneven, possibly bewitched, zigzag (see page 137 for the pattern). The background pieces for the witches, in strong lime green, have simply been cut out with scissors, and therefore the edges are a bit jagged and not quite straight.

I then cut out fabric pieces in dark, almost black fabrics, and appliquéd on small patches of lime green with an uneven zigzag.

The blocks were then sewn together, so that they overlapped by about ⅜in (10mm), with right side against wrong side. Therefore some of the raw edges are visible on the right side.

This quilt is freehand machine quilted, with the seam going in different directions and taking on different shapes. Since the quilt was sewn in a somewhat unusual way, it was also given a different kind of binding. What could it be, other than embroidered witches' stitches?

Finished size:
21½ x 18½in (54.5 x 47cm)

Flying the Broom

This atmospheric piece is great fun to stitch and full of lively colour contrasts. The appliqué patterns are on pages 137–139.

Finished size: *32 x 40in (81.3 x 102cm)*

Stitch as follows for the witch panel:

- Pick out four different fabrics of the same lightness/darkness for the background to the witch.
- Use the measurements in diagram 1 to cut them out, and sew the pieces together, as shown. The measurements include seam allowances.
- Put a ruler measuring 15 x 15in (38 x 38cm) on the piece, but place it a little askew so that one corner of the ruler hits the top edge of the piece and the other corner on the ruler hits the right-hand edge.
- Cut off the right-hand edge and what you are able to from the top and bottom edge.
- Move the ruler by pulling it towards the left-hand side. The corner of the ruler should hit the left-hand side and the bottom edge.
- Cut off the rest of the top and bottom edges and finally the left-hand edge, as in diagram 2. The piece should now look like diagram 3 and measure 20 x 15in (50.8 x 38cm).
- Make the broom handle from 15in (38cm) bias binding, which you fold out and iron with wrong sides together. Place the broom handle slightly diagonally on the background, 1½in (3.8cm) from the right-hand edge, with 8in (20.3cm) from the front end of the handle to the lower edge and 4in (10cm) from the broom end of the handle to the bottom edge. Sew the broom handle on with a straight seam. Cut away some of the seam allowance and fold the bias binding across so that it covers the remaining seam allowance. Sew the bias binding down by hand, only leaving raw edges at either end of the broom handle.
- The broom twigs are sewed with cotton yarn in a narrow zigzag.
- Appliqué the witch by hand, using freezer paper (see page 7). Darkish clothes will look good on her.

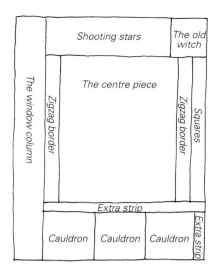

The background to the witch
Diagram 1

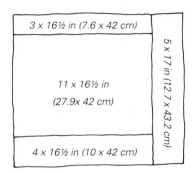

Diagram 2

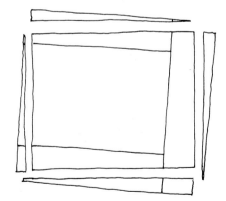

Diagram 3

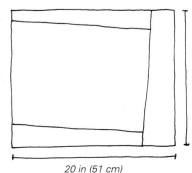

Stitch as follows for the houses, tree and cat:

- Sew together three squares measuring 8 x 8in (20.3 x 20.3cm) as background for the houses, tree and cat. The fabrics must be of the same lightness/darkness as the those in the background to the witch.
- Join the squares to the lower edge of the witch's background and trim off any excess.
- Cut out the houses, the tree and the cat using interfacing (see page 6) and appliqué them on with your machine (patterns on pages 138–139). The witch with her houses, tree and cat make up the centre piece.

Stitch as follows for the zigzag edge:

- Cut out squares measuring 3¼ x 3¼in (8.2 x 8.2cm) in five orange and five dark fabrics. Put each orange against a dark colour, right sides together, and follow the procedure from point 2 to point 5 on page 34.
- Trim the squares to 2¾ x 2¾in (7 x 7cm).
- Sew them together into a zigzag edge.
- Use the same procedure for the zigzag edge on the other side, only replace the five orange fabrics with five lime green ones.
- Sew on the zigzag edges along each side of the centre piece.
- On the outside of the right-hand zigzag edge, sew on a row of ten squares, each 2¾ x 2¾in (7 x 7cm). They should be a dark colour.

Stitch as follows for the cauldrons:

This procedure will give you four cauldrons.

- **A:** Cut two squares in background fabric (orange) and two squares in cauldron fabric (dark), measuring 4 x 4in (10 x 10cm).
- Iron them with right sides together, one orange against one dark and trace the diagonal on the orange fabric.
- Follow the procedure for the star block from point 3 to point 5 on page 34. Trim the squares to 3½ x 3½in (9 x 9cm).
- **B:** Cut two squares in lime green and two in background fabric (orange), measuring 5 x 5in (12.7 x 12.7cm).
- Iron them right sides together, and trace one horizontal and one vertical line and both diagonals through the centre, on the lightest fabric.
- Sew along each side of the diagonal lines with a seam allowance of ¼in (7mm) and then cut up in the horizontal, vertical and diagonal lines.

- Press and trim the pieces to 2 x 2in (5 x 5cm).
- **C:** Cut out one 5in (12.7cm) square in the background fabric (orange) and one square in a dark cauldron fabric. Follow the procedure for B.
- **D:** Cut out eight squares (six if you only want three cauldrons, as in the picture) in an orange background fabric, measuring 2 x 2in (5 x 5cm).
- **E:** Cut out eight rectangles (six if only three cauldrons) in an orange background fabric, measuring 2 x 4in (5 x 10cm).
- **F:** Cut out eight squares (six if only three cauldrons) in dark fabrics, measuring 5½ x 5½in (14 x 14cm). Cut them diagonally once and sew them on to the cauldron at the end.
- Sew together the cauldrons following the diagram below and trim to 9 x 9 (23 x 23cm).
- You will now have four cauldrons. Only three are needed for the wall hanging so you could use the fourth as a name tag on the back of the hanging.
- Once three cauldrons have been trimmed and sewn together, measure the width of the parts you have made so far. If the row of cauldrons is too short, just sew on a strip at one end.
- Don't sew the cauldrons on the rest of the wall hanging just yet; first check whether you need an extra strip to fill in between the cauldrons and the centre piece. You will know this once you know the length of the row of windows.

Cauldron block

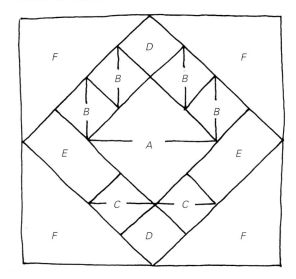

Stitch as follows for the old witch:

The old witch watching from the top corner can be sewn on with paper or thin interfacing, as follows.

- Trace the witch (pattern on page 137) in two parts on non-fusible interfacing or some other suitable fabric/paper. Her hat and face should be completed separately before the pieces are sewn together.
- Put a coarsely cut-out piece of fabric for the witch's hat or face with the wrong side down on the paper (part no. 1) and fasten it with a pin.
- The next part, no. 2, can also be coarsely cut out and is put against the fabric in part 1 with right sides together.
- Turn the interfacing/paper and sew together parts 1 and 2 in the line drawn between 1 and 2. Cut away some seam allowance if there is too much.
- Fold out part 2 and fasten it with a pin.
- Sew on parts 3, 4 and 5 in the same way.
- When both the face and the hat are finished, trim all the seam allowances and sew them together in the hat brim.
- Frame the witch in two rounds of Log Cabin and tear off the paper.

Stitch as follows for the shooting stars and sky:

- Cut out strips of 1½–2in (3.8–5cm) in half the fabric width.
- Join up the strips into two pieces that are about 10–13in (25–33cm) high.
- Cut up these new fabric pieces by putting the ruler at a slight angle, so that the pieces don't end up identical and with 90 degree angles.
- Cut up thin triangles for the shooting stars, about 1½in (3.8cm) at the widest and about 10in (25.5cm) long, but all of different length and width.
- Sew the shooting stars between the new fabric pieces, but not too close to the lower edge. Trim before you sew together each time, so that you have a clean, straight line to sew along. You should also iron after each sewn-on piece. The sky with the stars should first be trimmed along its lower edge, but don't cut off the tip of any shooting star. Join the sky to the old witch. Now join this panel to the top of the main panel, using the photograph on page 57 as your guide.

Stitch as follows for the windows:

- To make one window, take one lime green piece of fabric for a window. The size of this piece will determine the size of the window. It might for instance be 3 x 6in (7.6 x 15.25cm). The measurement isn't all that important, as long as the lines are straight. Cut the fabric into four parts (see the first diagram below).
- Cut strips in a dark fabric that measure, e.g, 1¼–2½in (3.2–6.3cm) for crossbars and frames for the window.
- Sew two window panes to each side of a strip, leaving a small gap for a crossbar, and press.
- Cut the strip by putting the ruler along the window panes. Cut off as little as possible from the panes (see second diagram below).
- Sew the panes and crossbar on a new strip (see third diagram below).
- Now the window only lacks a frame. Trim all four sides of the window.
- Sew a frame around all four sides of the window.
- Trim the windows when you have sewn as many as you need. They should be the same width but have different heights. You will probably need five or six windows for your wall hanging. I can't be more exact, since all the windows will turn out differently. The row of windows will also determine how high your wall hanging will be. If the window column is too long, you just cut off the excess, and if it is too short, add an extra piece. The window column is the last bit to be sewn on the wall hanging.
- Machine quilt the wall hanging freehand, and you might well want to use text as part of the quilting seam, sewing words like 'cauldron', 'shooting star', 'this wall hanging has been made by (name)', or something like that. Just use your imagination and let yourself go. If you have never done freehand quilting before, this would be a good opportunity to have a go.

Windows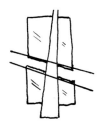

Bewitched Wall Hanging

If you think that last wall hanging looked like too much work, maybe this one would suit you better?

Cut out the tree in a mystical colour, with the houses and the moon in colours that go well with it, and appliqué them on a dark, spooky background. First frame the background in a lime green fabric. Then, to emphasize the spooky aspect of your wall hanging, put your ruler a little at an angle and cut a little bit off all four sides. Use your sewing machine for the appliqué (patterns on pages 138–139) and the quilting, and this wall hanging might be on your wall before you know it.

Finished size: *12 x 12in (30.5 x 30.5cm)*

Quilt As You Go

I found an article about this technique in an old American quilting magazine. What I found fascinating me was the way it had been sewn. The blocks were completed with batting and quilted one by one before they were sewn together. It reminded me of Japanese paper-folding techniques and folded patchwork.

It dawned on me fairly soon that if I were to make this kind of quilt, I would have to change the technique a little. This was done, and I have now made two quilts. One has little blocks and has been quilted and sewn together by hand (shown right), while the other has larger blocks and has been quilted and sewn together with a machine (shown overleaf). But the procedure is the same for both quilts.

The quilt consists of 153 blocks. It is 9 blocks wide and 17 blocks high. Each square for a block should measure about 4 x 4in (10 x 10cm).

I chose to make my quilt in dark colours combined with some that were clear and a bit sharp. It starts off in the centre with pastel versions of the colours, and then grows outwards, colour by colour. Grey, black, dark brown, dark green and dark blue are the dark colours in the quilt. The blocks are positioned with dark against dark and light against light, these again making up a square.

Finished size:
44 x 82¾in (112 x 210cm)
One block: 4⅞ x 4⅞in (12.3 x 12.3cm)

Stitch as follows:

- Sew together two and two 4in (10cm) squares, light against dark, or, as in one of my quilts, sharp against dark. Put them on top of each other with right sides together, with light against dark, diagram 1. Use any seam allowance you like, but make sure it is consistent for all the blocks.
- Sew together along short side – long side – short side in one operation, leaving one long side open, diagram 2. Fasten the seam at both ends.
- Holding the rectangle, open long side up, push the short side seams together. Pin this long diagonal seam together and then sew from the corner to a little past the middle, fasten the seam, skip a 2in (5cm) wide opening, start again with fastening stitches and continue sewing right into the corner, diagram 3.
- Cut a little off each corner seam allowance.
- Press the seams down gently with your fingers.
- Put the block down on the table and measure it with the ruler on top. Draw this measurement on a piece of fabric that is light coloured and without any pattern, so that your line is clearly visible. Also make a note of the measurement in figures plus the size of the square you are cutting up. The more information you write down, the better. The light piece of fabric will be useful when you press the block, and it will also contain all your measurements and information. If you have to leave this technique aside for a while, it will make it easy for you to pick up from where you left off.
- Cut out a piece of batting with the same measurements as the block, diagram 4.
- Fasten the batting with pins in the seam allowance of all four corners. Let the pin point towards the corner but not go beyond it.
- Turn the block with the pins the right way out. Use a knitting needle or similar to give the corners the right shape, diagram 5.
- Remove the pins one by one, and fasten them on the outside in the same corner as they came from. Make sure all the pins are removed.
- Sew the opening closed by hand.
- To make sure all the blocks turn out the same size, use the light piece of fabric as a template when you do the pressing. If you are sewing and quilting your quilt together by hand, follow the next two points.
- Draw up quilting lines ½in (1.2cm) either side

of the seams, i.e. in a double diagonal cross, diagram 6.
- Decide how to position the blocks in the quilt, and sew them together with staggered whipstitches (see diagram, right).
- If sewing and quilting your quilt together by machine, work as follows. When machine quilting, use the upper feed-dogs with a ruler. Adjust the ruler so that the seam will be 1½in (3.8cm) away from the edge. Quilt along all four sides with a continuous seam, forming a square on the block.
- Fasten a button in the middle of the block.
- Sew the blocks together with an embroidery stitch that secures both blocks when they are put edge to edge.

Diagram 1

 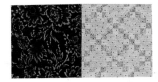

Diagram 2 *Diagram 3*

Diagram 4 *Diagram 5*

 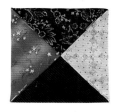

Diagram 6

Staggered whipstitches

Bag-Making Techniques

This section of the book is filled with all sorts of fabulous bags. Some of these have features in terms of assembly, handles, bottom or pockets. I will therefore explain this in the next few pages, so that you can easily find the correct procedure. In all instructions where this applies, I refer to these pages. Refer back to pages 6 and 7 for general advice on patchwork and quilting.

Assembling the Carryall and Purse

Carryall:
- Measure the carryall/purse and cut lining to the same size.
- If you want a pocket on the inside of the carryall, it must be sewn onto the right side of the lining now.
- Fold both the carryall and the lining double, right sides together, put them on top of each other and sew them together in the side seams with a ¼in (7mm) seam allowance.
- Put your hand into the carryall/purse itself (not the lining), and turn the model inside out.
- Complete the assembly following the pattern for your particular model.

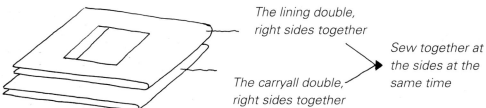

The lining double, right sides together

The carryall double, right sides together

Sew together at the sides at the same time

Sewing a corner:

- Sew the side seams, and if necessary also the bottom seam, with a seam allowance of ¼in (7mm).
- The raw edges may be sealed with a zigzag seam or covered with a strip of fabric. The strip should be 1½in (3.8cm) wide and must also be included in the side seams.
- It can then be folded across the raw edge and sewn down by hand.
- On some of the models, the bottom is made in a different fabric. In that case the bottom corners are folded and sewn by putting the side seam in the middle of the bottom fabric and everything is sewn together with a seam allowance of ¼in (7mm). The raw edges may either be sealed with a zigzag seam or covered with a strip of fabric as for the side seam.
- If the corner is not included in the pattern, it can be folded by putting the side seam in the middle of the bottom. Then a seam is sewn straight across the corner. You will find the length from the tip on the pattern you are using.
- The raw edges may either be sealed with a zigzag seam or covered with a strip of fabric as for the side seam. Complete the rest of the assembly following the pattern for your particular model.

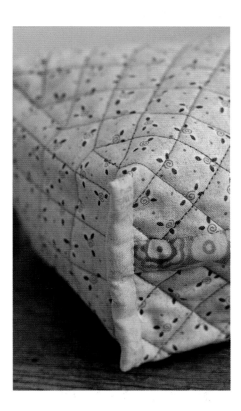

A fold in the side seam:

- Make the bottom by folding it up and between each side of the bag. Then include it in the side seams. Study the diagram below carefully and put the bag right sides together.
- Fold the bottom up between each side of the bag, so that folds are made. The size of the fold is given on each pattern.
- Stitch the side seams with a seam allowance of ¼in (7mm). Seal raw edges with a zigzag seam or cover it with a strip of fabric. The strip should be 1½in (3.8cm) wide and included in the side seams.
- Fold it over the raw edge and sew it down by hand.
- Complete the assembly following the pattern for your particular model.

Folded bottom:

- Sew the bag together so that it forms a cylinder.
- Seal the raw edges with a zigzag seam or sew a strip of fabric into the seam. The strip should be 1½in (3.8cm) wide, included in the stitching, folded over the raw edge and fastened with small hand stitches.
- The bottom of the model is created by folding in folds from either side, see the diagram below. The size of the fold will be given on each pattern.
- Stitch the seam and seal it with a zigzag. Make sure the side seam doesn't get stuck in the fold, but put it along one of the bag's long sides.
- Complete the assembly following the pattern for your particular model.

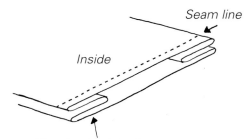

Seam line

Inside

The depth of the fold will vary depending on how wide the bottom should be. The deeper the fold, the wider the bottom.

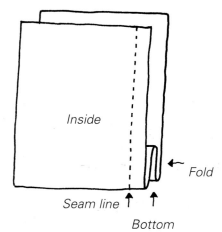

Inside

← *Fold*

Seam line ↑ ↑

Bottom

Pockets

Pocket with zip:

I have used this pocket on many models, both on the inside and the outside. There is one thing to keep in mind, however: the pocket must be sewn on the outside of the bag or on the lining, *before* the bag and the lining are sewn together.

You might also like to sew the top of the pocket into the top binding of the bag. The pocket will then end up on the inside of the bag.

- Make the pocket from a piece of fabric measuring 11½ x 7in (29.2 x 17.8cm) if you want the large size. I used this size on the outside of the Big Red Tote (page 78) and as a pocket on the Wool Fabric Bag (page 76), where the fabric measures 11 x 6in (28 x 15.2cm). On the wool models I have used a seam allowance of ½in (1.2cm).
- On each short side, fold and press a hem of about ½in (1.2cm).
- Sew in a zip on these two short sides. If you think this looks difficult, use a zip that is a bit longer than the short sides. That will make it easier to sew it in place. Put the zip along the edge of the short sides and stitch it into place.
- Turn the pocket inside out.
- Place the pocket so that the zip is about 1in (2.5cm) from the fold. This fold will be the top of the pocket.
- Leave the zip half open, stitch the side seams and turn the pocket out through the zip.
- Press the pocket gently to make it look flat and neat.
- Now sew the pocket onto

the bag, either horizontally or vertically, stitching along three sides. You will then have two pockets in one, one with a zip and one without.
- Make sure you attach the pocket to the bag before you join it up with the lining.

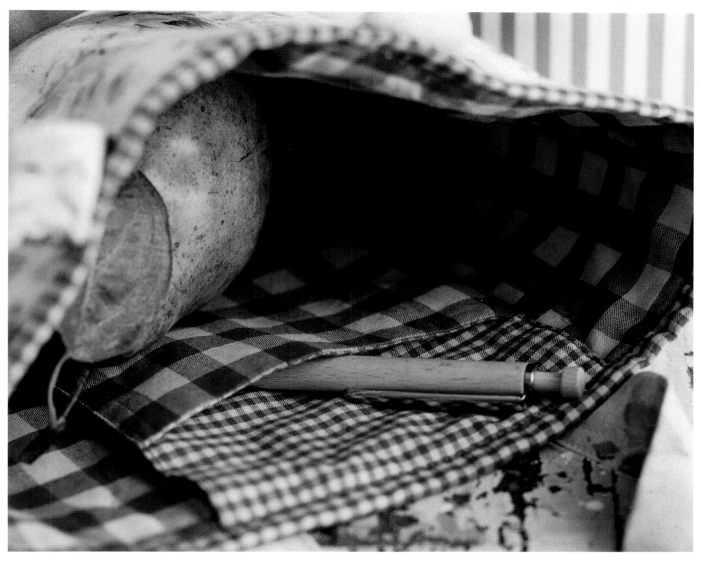

Inside pocket:

On nearly all the models you can also attach a pocket when the top binding is stitched on. The size is up to you. I have used three different sizes on my models.

- Make the pocket by cutting up two pieces of fabric measuring 11 x 5½in (28 x 14cm) for a large bag, or 10 x 5in (25.4 x 12.7cm) for a small bag, or 7 x 4in (17.8 x 10cm) for a make-up bag.
- Put the pieces right sides together and sew them together along the two long sides and one short side.
- Turn the pieces inside out and press neatly with an iron, making sure the corners are clearly defined.
- Make a pocket by folding up the short side about 4in (10cm) and sewing down the sides to create a pocket.
- Include the pocket in the top binding.

Handles

I use mostly handles that I make myself. Then I get both the colours and lengths that match my new bag. But you can also buy many nice handles, and I have used some for my bags. If you prefer to make your own handles, however, here are some ways to do it.

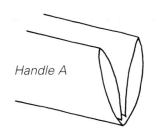

Handle A

Handle A:

- Cut a strip that is four times as wide as you want the handle to be. The length will vary from model to model. You will find the measurements with the instructions for each model.
- Iron it folded double, wrong sides together.
- Open the strip and fold the long sides in towards the ironed edge in the middle.
- Fold it back into the first pressed edge (see the small diagram above).
- Cut a strip of batting the length and width of the finished handle. If you use thick batting, this should be cut a little smaller than the finished handle, so that the batting will fit inside the handle. Use double batting if you want a thick handle.
- Put the batting inside the handle and hold it all in place with sewing pins across the handle.
- Stitch once or twice along both edges of the handle.
- Attach the handle as in the instructions for your model.

Handle A can also be made without any batting, but it will then look thinner and be more floppy.

Handle B:

This handle can be made with or without batting, depending on the look you are after.

- Cut a strip twice as wide as you want the handle to be. The length will vary from bag to bag. The measurements are with the instructions for each model.
- Cut a strip of batting that is the length and width of the finished handle. If you want a thick handle, use double batting.
- Iron the fabric for the handle folded double lengthwise and put the batting in between. Sew a stitch about ³⁄₁₆in (5mm) from the folded edge of the handle.
- Then cut a strip of 1½in (3.8cm) for each handle, with the same length as the handle.
- This strip is sewn onto the handle as a binding or as a bias binding over the raw edge.
- At the end of each handle you

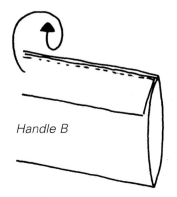

Handle B

can sew on a small piece of fabric, 1½ x 2½in (3.8 x 6.3cm) and fold it double over the raw edge before sewing it on by hand. You only need to do this if the handle end will be visible.

Handle C:

On some of the models I have used a handle made of two different fabrics. It has no batting, so it is light and not equally suitable for all types of bags.

- Find two different fabrics that look good with your bag. Cut a strip 1¾in (4.4cm) in the one fabric and a strip 2½in (6.3cm) in the other.
- Put the strips right sides together and sew a seam along each edge, about ¼in (7mm) from the edge.
- Turn the handle the right way out and press it in such a way that the widest strip comes round to the other side. Now stitch along this and the other edge of the handle.

Binding

I have finished off most of my models with a top binding. I have done it on bags, toilet bags and make-up bags.

- Sew a strip 1½in (3.8cm) wide to the top edge of the bag. Put it with the right side against the inside of the bag and machine stitch it on about ¼in (7mm) from the edge.
- Fold the strip across to the outside of the bag and machine stitch it on.

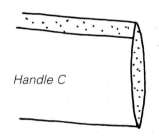

Handle C

Bottom Plate

If you prefer the bottom of your bag a little firmer, a loose piece of cardboard may be put there. I make a bottom plate for all my flat-bottomed bags, including the bigger toilet bags.

- Measure the bottom, cut out three or four pieces of cardboard of the right size and glue them together to make the plate stiff enough. You could use the cardboard from a cereal box.
- Sew a pocket in a fabric that matches the inside of the bag. Make the pocket 2in (5cm) longer than the bottom measurement, and keep the pocket open at one of the short sides.
- Insert the cardboard into the pocket, and fold in the opening.

Zip Fasteners

Some of the bags have a zip sewn into the opening. There are zips in all the make-up bags and toilet bags. I have used the sewing machine for all the zips, with the exception of the little make-up bags which have a curved opening. On them the zip has been sewn in by hand. All the models that have a zip have first been finished with a sealing edge, and then the zip is sewn on.

By sewing machine:
- Open the zip and pin it to the bag by the first 'tooth' about ½in (1.2cm) from the side seam and finish about ½in (1.2cm) from the other side seam. Work first on one side of the bag, then on the other. Make sure the zip is put in straight, so that the two sides fit together when you close the zip.
- Start sewing in the zip from the side seam where you have the end of the zip. Let the seam run right in the edge of the binding. Sew the zip around the entire opening and finish by the side seam where you started.
- On the inside of the bag, fasten the zip using little whipstitches. If the zip is too long, cut it off, but first sew right across the zip teeth close to where you are going to cut. Then use small hand stitches to neatly fasten the end of the zip.

By hand:
- Open up the zip and pin one side of it to the inside of the make-up bag.
- Thread a needle with a double thread and start sewing small stitches from the inside. These stitches are a bit like small backstitches. You put the needle through the zip and into the make-up bag, but not so far that the stitch will show on the outside of the bag. Then you push the needle up about ⅛in (3mm) from where it went down. Let the next stitch go down slightly further over than where the first stitch came up, and so on.
- Repeat on the other side. Make sure the zip is put in straight, so that the two sides fit together when you close the zip.
- On the inside of the bag, fasten the zip using little whipstitches. If the zip is too long, cut it off when the side seam has been stitched.

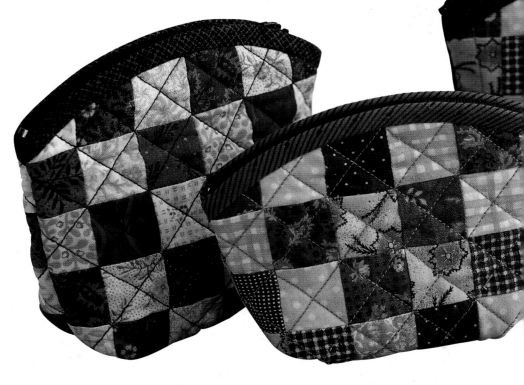

Flat Bags

I have made two bags that are rather different from the others. The only similarity is the yo-yo decoration, which you will also find on the model Two in One on page 100.

The Grey Bag

- Cut two pieces of fabric 12 x 25in (30.5 x 63.5cm), one in linen and the other in a cotton that goes well with the linen.
- Cut a piece of batting 9½ x 25in (24 x 63.5cm) – I have used synthetic table batting.
- Put the batting against the wrong side of the cotton centrally so that there is an equal amount of fabric on each long side of the batting.
- Press the excess fabric over the batting and place it batting side down in the middle of the right side of the linen. Secure with a few pins before tacking the layers together.
- Sew the linen fabric, batting and cotton fabric together by hand using whipstitches and embroidery thread.
- Sew on a few pretty buttons for decoration.
- Fold the bag right sides together and sew the side seams with a seam allowance of ¼in (7mm).
- Turn the bag the right way out and press lightly with an iron.
- Fold the top edge double, altogether 1¾in (4.4cm) and machine stitch in place about ¾in (2cm) from the edge.
- Put the bag down flat and sew a machine seam along each side, in the edge of the cotton fabric. The bag will be smaller than it looks, but this seam hides the seam allowance.
- Attach two wooden handles with black cords. Fasten the cords with the machine, then tie on the handles.

The Turquoise Bag

- Cut two linen pieces 15½ x 27in (39.4 x 68.5cm), one turquoise, one lime green.
- Cut one piece of batting 12 x 27in (30.5 x 68.5cm). I used synthetic table batting.
- Put the batting on the wrong side of the lime green piece centrally so there is an equal amount of linen on each long side of the batting.
- Press the excess fabric on top of the batting and place it with the batting side down in the middle of the right side of the turquoise linen. It's a good idea to fasten this with a few pins before tacking it together.
- Sew the turquoise linen, batting and lime green linen together using a machine embroidery stitch, preferably with a thread that is clearly visible.
- Make three yo-yos (see page 141). Put a glass bead in the middle of each yo-yo and sew them on as decorations.
- Fold the bag right sides together and sew the side seams with a seam allowance of ¼in (7mm).
- Turn the bag the right way out and press lightly with an iron.
- Fold the top edge double, altogether 1¾in (4.4cm), and machine stitch in place about ¾in (2cm) from the edge.
- Put the bag down flat and sew a machine seam along each side, in the edge of the lime green linen. The bag will be smaller than it looks, but the machine seam hides the seam allowance.
- The handles are made as in the instructions for Handle A on page 70 with double batting.
- The handles are ¾in (2cm) wide and 35½in (90cm) long.
- The handles are looped through each other at the top and then attached to the bag with a couple of seams 2in (5cm) from the edge of the bag. Fold in about ½in (1.2cm) at each end of the handle before stitching them on. The distance between the handles is 6½in (16.5cm).

Wool Fabric Bags

These two stylish bags are made in lightweight wool fabrics in check and herringbone patterns, with smart leather handles.

Wool Tote

- Cut two lengths of 33 x 8½in (84 x 21.6cm) in different fabrics.
- Sew them together along one long edge with a ½in (1.2cm) seam allowance to make one piece about 33 x 16½in (84 x 42cm). Press the seam allowance open.
- Cut out fabric for two pockets, each 11 x 6in (28 x 15.2cm).
- Follow the procedure for a zip pocket on page 73 and sew them on the bag by machine. Place them alongside the seam with the zip horizontally on one pocket and vertically on the other.
- I have also sewn one zip pocket on the lining.
- Follow the procedure for making this carryall on page 64; page 71 tells you how to bind the top edge.
- Once the binding has been sewn on, fold it across to the inside and stitch it down.
- I made the handles for this bag out of leftover leather pieces. The leather was cut into strips of 11 x 1¼in (28 x 3.2cm) and folded double lengthways. I stitched along the edge, but not but not right to the ends because the ends were easier to sew on flat. Sew the handles on about 3in (7.6cm) apart.

Small Wool Tote

- Cut out a length of 25 x 2½in (63.5 x 6.3cm) in one fabric, and a length of 25 x 9in (63.5 x 23cm) in another fabric.
- Sew them together along one long edge with a ½in (1.2cm) seam allowance to make one piece about 25 x 10½in (63.5 x 26.7cm). Press the seam allowance open.
- Follow the procedures for making a carryall on page 64 and for how to attach a binding around the top edge on page 71.
- I have sewn a handy zip pocket on the lining.
- I made the handles for this bag out of leftover leather pieces. The leather was cut into strips of 11 x 1¼in (28 x 3.2cm) and folded double lengthways. I then stitched along the edge, but not but not right to the ends because the ends were easier to sew on flat. Sew the handles on about 3in (7.6cm) apart.

Patchwork Totes

If you think these patchwork bags look a lot like the bags in wool on the previous pages, you would be correct. The difference here is that I have joined up bits of fabric the way we quilters do, and voila! a patchwork bag.

Big Red Tote

- Cut out eight light and eight dark rectangles, each 2½ x 6½in (6.3 x 16.5cm).
- Sew them into two rows of eight patches, alternating light and dark colours, as shown in the picture.
- Cut out two pieces of 10½ x 16½in (26.7 x 42cm) in red fabric and sew them together with the rows of rectangles to make two pieces.
- Join the two pieces into one. This seam will form the bottom of the bag.
- Quilt together the bag and cotton batting, using a straight machine seam.
- Trim the batting to fit the size of the bag.
- Cut out one pocket in striped red fabric, 11 x 6in (28 x 15.2cm).
- Follow the procedure for making a pocket with a zip on page 68, and machine it on the bag. Place the pocket in the middle of one of the red pieces. There is only one outside pocket.
- Follow the procedure for making this carryall on page 64 and bind the top edge as explained on page 71.
- The bag has an inside pocket – see page 69. I have chosen the bigger size pocket.
- The handles are 22in (56cm) long and are made as Handle C on page 71.
- Fold in ½in (1.2cm) at each end of the handles and secure them to the outside of the bag with a machine seam. Put a button at each end of the handles for decoration and reinforcement. The distance between the handles is 4½in (11.5cm).

Little Blue Tote

- Cut out ten light and ten dark rectangles, each 2½ x 6½in (6.3 x 16.5cm).
- Sew them into one large piece, five pieces wide and four pieces long and alternating light and dark pieces (see the photo below).
- Quilt together the bag and cotton batting, using a straight machine seam.
- Trim the batting to fit the size of the bag.
- Cut out one pocket in the same fabric as for the lining, 11 x 6in (28 x 15.2cm).
- Make a pocket with a zip as explained on page 68, and machine it on the lining.
- Follow the procedure for making this carryall on page 64 and bind the top edge as explained on page 71.
- You can attach the handles while sewing on the top binding.
- The handles are 12in (30cm) long and made like handle C on page 71. If you think the handle is too wide, fold it and sew it down by machine.
- Put the handles on the inside, underneath the top binding. The distance between the handles is 3in (7.6cm).
- Before sewing on the binding on the outside, fold up the handles to keep them out of the way of the machine.

Little Tote with Flowers

This is the sister of the Little Blue Tote. I have used the same procedure, but exchanged the patchwork for a whole piece of fabric measuring 11 x 25in (28 x 63.5cm).

The piece has been machine quilted with batting in wavy lines horizontally and vertically.

Cut the batting to the same size as the bag. The handles are a little different – 17in (43cm) long, with a finished width of 1in (2.5cm). Cut them out as 17 x 4in (43 x 10cm) and then follow the instructions for handle A without batting on page 70.

Fold in ½in (1.2cm) at each end of the handles and sew them on the bag. The distance between the handles is 2¾in (7cm). If you like, sew on some buttons to decorate the handles.

Kari Anne's Flowers

Kari Anne has lent me a bag which she made out of denim. She has been really creative, quilting lovely large flowers freehand with the machine. The bag has been assembled in the same way as the carryall on page 64.

This bag measures 15¾ x 17½in (40 x 44.4cm) and the top binding is part of the lining, which she has folded over onto the right side and fastened with a seam. The handles are attached in the same seam.

Bags and Buttons

I collect buttons and keep a small store. Whenever a garment is thrown out I first remove the buttons and any nice labels. If I am also able to reuse the fabric, so much the better! For these models I have only used buttons from my own store, while the fabrics are new and not of the normal patchwork kind. I have used narrow-striped corduroy and coarsely woven cotton fabrics and made them into a tote bag, a flat purse and a toilet bag.

Big Tote

- Cut out eight light and ten dark squares of 6½ x 6½in (16.5 x 16.5cm).
- Sew them into two pieces that are three patches wide and three high, alternating light and dark pieces (see photo, right).
- Sew the two pieces together. This seam will form the bottom of the bag.
- Quilt the bag and cotton batting together with buttons. You can use the sewing machine and put buttons on all the seams. Don't add the buttons nearest the top before the handles have been sewn on.
- Trim the batting to the same size as the bag.
- Cut out one pocket in the same fabric as the lining, 11 x 6in (28 x 15.2cm).
- Follow instructions on page 68 for making a pocket with a zip, and machine it to the lining.
- Complete the carryall following the instructions on page 64 and bind the top as explained on page 71.
- The handles are 26in (66cm) long and 1½in (3.8cm) wide when finished. Follow the instructions for making Handle B on page 71.
- Attach the handles a bit below the top and in the row of buttons – how far down is up to you! The handles are fairly long and may not suit all sizes.
- Complete your bag by sewing on the final buttons.

Flat Purse

- Cut out four light and four dark squares 5 x 5in (12.7 x 12.7cm).
- Sew them into one piece that is two patches wide and four high, alternating light and dark pieces (see the photo, right).
- Quilt together the purse and cotton batting with buttons. You can use the machine and put buttons on all the seams.
- Trim the batting to the same size as the purse.
- Make the purse in the same way as the carryall on page 64 and bind the top as explained on page 71.
- To add a zip, follow the instructions on page 73 using your sewing machine.

Toilet Bag

- Cut out six light and six dark squares 5 x 5in (12.7 x 12.7cm).
- Sew them into two pieces that are two patches high and four wide, alternating light and dark pieces (see the photo, right).
- Cut a bottom piece, 9½ x 4½in (24 x 11.5cm) and sew it on between the two patch pieces.
- Quilt together the toilet bag and the cotton batting with buttons. You can use the machine and put buttons on all the seams.
- Trim the batting to the same size as the bag.
- Cut out a lining the same size as the bag.
- Sew the two side seams on both the bag and the lining and leave them wrong side out.
- Fold each corner at the bottom of both the bag and the lining by putting the side seam in the middle of the bottom fabric.
- Place the corner of the lining on top of the corner of the bag and sew them together with a seam allowance of ¼in (7mm). This seam keeps the lining in place.
- Turn your bag the right way out and bind the top as explained on page 71. To add the zip, follow the instructions on page 73.

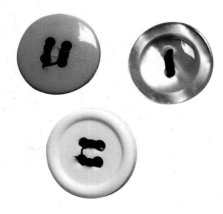

Triangles Bag

This smart bag is easily made with remnants, or would be the perfect excuse to buy new fabric – if you need one!

Many stores and mail-order companies sell a good range of ready-made handles.

- Make a template by following the diagram below.
- Use the template to cut out 30 light and 30 dark triangles. Sew them together, alternating light and dark colours, in six rows.
- Cut out six rectangles of 13⅛ x 3in (33.5 x 7.6cm) in fabric that looks good with the triangles. Place the rows of triangles and the rectangles alternately and sew them together into one large piece.
- For the bottom of the bag, cut out a piece 30½ x 2¾in (77.5 x 7cm) of the same fabric as the rectangles and sew it onto the piece you already have. This makes up the whole bag.
- Quilt the bag with batting and backing on the machine, using straight seams. You may need to trim a little more once you have quilted, but make sure you don't cut too much off the triangles.
- Follow the instructions for making a folded bottom on page 66. The fold measures 2½in (6.3cm).
- The handles for the bag were bought in a patchwork shop and may be attached to the bag with fabric loops. The loops are attached to the binding on the outside of the bag. The loops are then threaded through the handle attachments and secured to the bag with buttons.
- Bind the top of the bag following the instructions on page 71.
- See page 72 if you want a plate to reinforce the bag bottom.

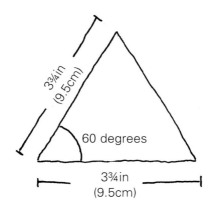

3¾in (9.5cm)

60 degrees

3¾in (9.5cm)

Green Linen Bag

This model is related to the Triangles Bag, opposite. They have the same measurements and procedure, but look quite different. The green bag is made out of a piece of linen, has fabric handles and a very different binding from the Triangles Bag. I'm more than happy to give you the measurements and instructions if you would like to have one too.

- Cut 32½ x 16in (82.5 x 40.6cm) in linen, batting and fabric for the inside.
- Now machine quilt the bag in diagonal, gently wavy lines using multicoloured thread. I also machine quilted rose names freehand. It's best to sew each name twice, in the same line, to make the writing show up a little more.
- Then follow the instructions for making a folded bottom on page 66. The fold measures 2½in (6.3cm).
- The handles are 28in (71cm) long and 1in (2.5cm) wide when finished. Follow the procedure for Handle A with batting on page 70.
- Attach the handles with pins from the inside of the bag before sewing the binding on. The distance between the handles is 5½in (14cm).
- The binding is 32½ x 9½in (82.5 x 24cm), sewn together into a cylinder and folded double.
- Pin the binding to the inside of the bag and sew it on with a seam allowance of ¼in (7mm).
- Turn the binding to the outside of the bag and press well.
- Page 72 explain how you can make an extra plate to reinforce the bottom of the bag.

Make-Up Case

- Cut two rectangles of 6 x 9in (15.2 x 23cm) in the fabric you used for the broad binding on the Green Linen Bag.
- Cut out a bottom piece, measuring 3½ x 9in (9 x 23cm) and sew it on in the middle of the two rectangles.
- Cut two strips for the edge of the makeup bag, 2 x 9in (5 x 23cm), in a red check fabric.
- Sew them onto each side of the make-up bag as an edge.
- Quilt the make-up bag with cotton batting and a fabric for the inside, using gently curved lines on the machine.
- Trim the batting to make it like the make-up bag.
- Follow the instructions for how to make a fold in the side seam on page 66. Bind the top edge as explained on page 71 and sew on the zip by machine as explained on page 73.

Little Roses

This charming bag, with its pretty, rose-strewn fabrics, is perfect for summer. The matching make-up bag is equally easy to stitch.

- Cut out eight 6in (15.2cm) squares and sew them together, three high and four wide.
- Cut the batting and lining to about 16 x 24in (40.6 x 61cm).
- Place the patchwork piece 3in (7.6cm) away from the edge of the longest side of the batting and lining.
- Machine quilt the whole piece with straight seams in a grid.
- Sew loops to hold the handles: cut out a strip 3 x 10in (7.6 x 25.5cm). Iron the strip double, wrong sides together. Fold and press the seam allowances on the long sides into the middle. Machine stitch together right at the edge. Cut the strip into four loops, each 2in (5cm) long.
- Place the four loops in the top edge of the bag, the first one 3in (7.6cm) from the edge, the next one 4in (10cm) further along. Repeat on the other side. This is where the handles will go, so do check that you have placed them correctly before sewing them in place.
- Sew on the loops together with a strip measuring 2 x 22½in (5 x 57cm) along the whole width of the bag.
- Press the loops and strip of fabric so that they cover the extra 3in (7.6cm) edge of the batting and lining.
- Trim the bag clean and follow the instructions for sewing a corner on page 65 and attaching a binding on page 71. Sew the corner seam 2in (5cm) in from

the tip of the corner.
- Make sure you thread the loops through the handle rings before sewing the binding.
- Page 72 explains how you can make a bottom plate to reinforce the bottom of the bag.

Rosy Make-Up Bag

- Cut out four rectangles 4½ x 5½in (11.5 x 14cm) in light rose fabrics. Sew them together into two pieces, each one rectangle high and two wide.
- Cut a piece for the bottom, 3½ x 7½in (9 x 19cm) and sew it on between the two patchwork pieces.
- Quilt the make-up bag with cotton batting and a lining fabric, sewing diagonal, gently curved lines with the machine. Trim only as strictly necessary.
- Follow the instructions for how to sew a corner on page 65, a binding around the top on page 71 and how to sew on a zip by machine on page 73.

Round-Handled Bags

Use fabrics from your fabric store for these attractive bags. Simple ready-made handles make the bags even quicker to complete.

All Squares

- Cut 42 light and 42 dark squares, each 3 x 3in (7.6 x 7.6cm). Place the squares so that light and dark ones alternate and sew them together into a piece that is six squares wide and 14 long.
- Press gently and cut a lining of the same size.
- Put the outside of the bag and the lining right sides together and sew 8in (20cm) long seams at each end of the length. These will be the splits at either side of the bag.
- Separate the outside and the lining and put the outside with right sides together and a fold in the bottom. Do the same with the lining.
- Stitch the side seams on both the outside and the lining.
- Turn the whole bag out through the opening so that the lining is placed correctly on the inside.
- Press lightly on the splits at either side of the bag and sew a seam along the splits.
- Seal the open short sides with a machine zigzag, taking in both the outside and the lining.
- Sew on a few buttons and fasten them both in the outside and the lining. This will keep the lining in place.
- Sew on the handles by folding a hem across each handle in order to sew on the hem by machine. Tack the hem down before sewing, because the bag will pucker once the handle is in place.

Bag With Rose

- Cut a rectangle of 15½ x 23in (39.5 x 58.5cm).
- Cut two strips of 15½ x 5¼in (39.5 x 13.3cm) in a fabric that looks good with the first one.
- Sew a strip to each short side of the main rectangle.
- Machine quilt the piece with cotton batting in diagonal, gently curved lines and trim.
- The bag is probably a little smaller than before it was quilted. It is therefore a good idea to measure the bag before cutting out the lining.
- Cut the lining according to your own measurements of the bag.
- Now follow point 3 to the end of the instructions for the All Squares bag, opposite.
- The bag is decorated with a fabric rose. The diagrams on page 140 show you how to make one.

The little make-up bag next to the green bag is made of a piece of fabric measuring 8 x 11in (20.3 x 28cm). Quilt the fabric with cotton batting and sew as for the carryall on page 64.

Flower Power

I might have had my younger days in mind when choosing the colours for this bag. The decoration is certainly a typical '70s flower. This bag may serve as a little greeting to those of us who are pleased to recall the days of flower power, long hair and women's lib.

- Cut a 31 x 17½in (78.7 x 44.4cm) rectangle in linen and a batting suitable for bag-making and machine quilting. The bag should also be stiff enough to stand upright.
- Machine quilt the bag in gently curved lines both horizontally and vertically. Use thread of a colour that is different from the linen if you prefer, for example an orange thread. This will make your seam stand out and be more decorative.
- Pin a square of 7½ x 7½in (19 x 19cm) to the front of the bag and sew it on with some of the quilting seams.
- Trace the flower (pattern on page 142) on double-sided iron-on interfacing (see page 6) and iron it onto the square at the front of the bag.
- Appliqué the flower freehand

with the machine by setting it to a straight seam, removing the bottom feed dogs and attaching the embroidery foot. Sew three rounds onto the flower, about ⅛in (2–3mm) inside the edge. Do some rounds in the middle of the flower as well. If you like, you can use the machine to write on the bag, for instance words like 'flower', 'sun', and maybe the name of the person you are making the bag for.
- Follow the instructions on page 66 for making a fold in the side seam. The fold is 2½in (6.3cm).
- Page 71 tells you how to make the binding and handles. The handles are 22½in (57cm) long and 1½in (3.8cm) wide when completed. Follow the instructions for making Handle B with double batting.

- On the inside of this bag I have also put a pocket with a zip, see page 68. It was sewn in place together with the binding.
- Fasten the handles on the inside of the bag by machine. The distance between the handles is 4in (10cm).
- Page 72 explains how you can make a bottom plate to reinforce the bottom of the bag.

Dramatic Totes

Black and Green

- Cut a strip of 1¼ x 11in (3.2 x 28cm) in a bright green fabric.
- Cut a strip 3 x 11in (7.6 x 28cm) in a black fabric with a white pattern.
- Cut two rectangles of 5½ x 11in (14 x 28cm) in two black fabrics with different white patterns.
- Repeat for the other side of the tote.
- Sew them into two parts, one for each side of the tote.
- For the bottom, cut out a rectangle measuring 4½ x 13¾in (11.5 x 35cm). Here, too, you can use a black fabric with a white pattern.
- Sew together the two parts of the tote with the bottom in the middle.
- Machine quilt the tote with cotton batting and a

lining fabric in gently curved lines horizontally and vertically.
- Trim, but don't cut off too much.
- Follow the instructions for making a fold in the side seam on page 66. The fold should measure 2in (5cm).
- Pages 70 and 71 tell you how to make the binding and the handle. The handle is 30in (76cm) long and 1¼in (3.2cm) wide when completed. Follow the instructions for Handle A with batting.
- Make the decoration before the handle is sewn on: cut a strip 1¼ x 13in (3.2 x 33cm). Iron the strip double, wrong sides together. Iron the seam allowance in towards the middle on both the long sides. Sew a machine seam right at the edge. Cut the strip into lengths of 4in (10cm) each. Join up each length into a small circle.
- Thread the circles onto the handle and fasten the handle on the outside of the tote, in each side, with a machine seam.
- Cut a piece of cord to make an 18in (46cm) loop, fold it double and tie two knots 2in (5cm) apart.
- Fasten the loop at the top edge of the tote on one side, preferably with the machine.
- Sew on a large button on the other side of the tote; it must fit the loop so that the tote can be closed.
- Page 72 explains how you can make a bottom plate to reinforce the bottom of the tote.

Black and Orange

I have also made the same tote with an orange strip and a zip (see the photograph left). You can sew on the zip by machine, as described on page 73. The handle is the same as the black and green version, but it has been attached diagonally across the tote and fastened with large buttons. The circle decorations on the handle have been omitted.

Sewing Bag

Sometimes I go out to do my sewing with others, and then it's nice to have all my bits and pieces in one place. I have made myself a bag which holds everything I need.

stitched two seams, which means that I have three pockets on each side of the bag.

- Then follow instructions for making a fold in the side seam on page 66. The fold should measure 2in (5cm).
- Pages 70 and 71 tell you how to make the binding and the handles. The handles are 21in (53.3cm) long and 1in (2.5cm) wide when completed. Follow the instructions for Handle A without batting.
- Fasten the handles with buttons on the outside of the bag.
- Page 72 explains how you can make a bottom plate to reinforce the bottom of the bag.

- Cut out 18 light and 18 dark squares each 2½ x 2½in (6.3 x 6.3cm).
- Sew them together, alternating light and dark patches to form two pieces (each three high, six wide), one for each side of the bag.
- Cut out a rectangle of 12½ x 5in (31.7 x 12.7cm) for the bottom.
- Sew one side panel to each long edge of the bottom piece.
- Cut out two strips of 12½ x 2in (31.7 x 5cm) for the edge. Sew the strips onto each short side of the bag.
- Quilt the bag with cotton batting

and fabric for the inside, along either side of each seam, using the machine. Trim, but don't cut too drastically.
- Cut out a piece to be used for pockets, 12½ x 16in (32 x 40.6cm).
- Fold in about ½in (1.2cm) twice in each side and sew down the hem by machine.
- Pin the fabric for the pockets to the inside of the bag. Place it in the middle, with the wrong side facing the inside of the bag.
- Make little pockets with machine seams from one side of the pocket fabric to the other. I

Two in One

This bag was made for the beach. When you set off from home, everything goes inside the bag - towel, swimming costume, and maybe a flask of coffee. When the day is over and you head home, take the green bag out of the plastic bag. With the wet things in the plastic bag, everything else stays nice and dry.

The plastic one

- Cut out two pieces of plastic each measuring 15½ x 31in (39.4 x 78.7cm).
- Page 141 explains how to make a yo-yo. There are 32 yo-yos on the plastic bag, 16 on each side with four rows and four columns. These will be placed between the plastic pieces and will be kept in place with vertical and horizontal seams.
- Draw a grid on the plastic with a hera marker or similar, with lines 2¾in (7cm) apart.
- Both sides of the bag must be decorated and sewn with yo-yos at the same time.
- Put the plastic pieces on top of each other and sew the middle horizontal seam first. Orange thread would look good.
- The next seam should be the one nearest to the bottom.
- Put in the two bottom yo-yos on either side of the middle seam and sew the next seam across.
- Continue in this way until you have two rows that are four yo-yos high.
- The next two seams will go on either side of the two rows of yo-yos.
- Sew the remaining seams across the fabric.
- Put in the remaining yo-yos on either side of the middle rows.
- Seal in the two outside rows of yo-yos with a seam each.
- Fold the bag double and sew both side seams.
- If you want the bag to stand

upright, fold in the corner by putting the side seam in the middle of the bottom. Then sew a seam across the corner. The measurement from the tip to the seam is 1½in (3.8cm).

- Cut out two handles in plastic, 1¼ x 27in (3.2 x 68.6cm) and sew them on while sewing a seam around the opening of the bag.

The green one

- Cut out 18 squares each 5½ x 5½in (14 x 14cm) in fresh green colours.
- Sew them together, three wide and six high.
- Quilt the piece for the bag with cotton batting and fabric for the inside. The seams can be machined in diagonal lines.
- Trim and fold it double, right sides together.
- Sew both side seams. They can either be sealed with a machine zigzag stitch or covered up with a strip of fabric. The strip should be cut 1½in (3.8cm) wide and be included in the side seams. Then fold it over the raw edge and sew down by hand.
- Pages 70 and 71 explain how to make the binding and the handles. The handles are 12in (30.5cm) long and ⅝in (1.6cm) wide when completed. Follow the instructions for Handle A without batting.
- Sew the handles on while sewing the binding around the opening. Attach the handles to the inside of the bag, which is best done when both the bags are together.

Fray Technique Bags

Three books ago I made a blanket in a technique I found in the US. This technique did not have a Scandinavian name, so I called it 'fray technique'. A number of people have tried this technique, and I have seen it referred to as 'fray technique' in several places. It is a simple technique and therefore right up my street. You sew the fabrics together with batting and lining, either in blocks or bigger parts of the quilt, and then join the blocks together with the seam allowance facing out. The seam allowances are then cut up and the whole piece is given a machine wash.

I have now tried a variation of this technique, where you sew together the blocks with the seam allowances on the right side, and then afterwards quilt with the batting and lining. Here, too, the seam allowances must be cut up and the whole thing is finally machine washed. I have made the bag in two versions, one with rainbow colours (opposite) and one with old checked shirts (on page 105). The bags are the same size. While I was in the fray technique mood I made a make-up bag as well (overleaf).

Rainbow Bag

- To make the bag, cut out nine strips each 2¼ x 14½in (5.7 x 36.8cm) for each side of the bag in rainbow colours or other colours to your liking.
- Sew the two sides separately with the seam allowances facing out, using a ½in (1.2cm) seam allowance.
- The bag narrows a bit towards the bottom. Use a ruler to draw a line from the top corner ending at the bottom line, 1½in (3.8cm) in from the bottom corner. Cut off the triangle outside the line.
- Cut fabric for the lining to the corresponding size.
- First put the bag parts wrong sides together on the fabric you have chosen for the lining and cut the lining to fit the bag.
- The batting goes between the layers of fabric. Cut it ½in (1.2cm) smaller than the fabrics all the way round. This corresponds to the size of the seam allowances.
- Put the lining wrong side up, then the batting and finally the outside of the bag with its wrong side facing the batting.

- To make the bottom of the bag, cut two pieces each 4 x 8½in (10 x 21.6cm), one in fabric for the outside and one in lining fabric.
- Cut one piece of batting, 3 x 7½in (7.6 x 19cm).
- Put batting between the pieces as for the bag and machine quilt the bottom.
- Sew the bag together, taking ½in (1.2cm) seam allowance all the way round. First sew the bottom onto the bag, then stitch the side seams and finally the corner seams. Cut notches into the sides of the bag to make it easier to sew the corner seams. Don't forget to keep the seam allowances on the outside of your bag!

- To make the bag handles, cut two fabric strips of 2¼ x 16in (5.7 x 40.6cm) and two strips of 2¼ x 11in (5.7 x 28cm). Cut two batting strips each 2¼ x 15in (5.7 x 38cm) for each handle.
- Put the batting between the fabrics, 1in (2.5cm) from the one end and 4in (10cm) from the other end. Put the shortest fabric strip right at the edge of one end. It will therefore be 4in (10cm) away from the other end. Tie these together.
- Sew on the handles by folding up the ends by 1in (2.5cm), so that they are attached to the outside of the bag. The distance between the handles is about 4in (10cm).
- Cut up the seam allowances with a pair of sharp scissors and wash your bag in the washing machine at 40 degrees centigrade.

Rainbow Make-Up Bag

Use the Rainbow Bag instructions on the previous page, but with different measurements.

- Cut out five strips 2¼ x 11in (5.7 x 28cm) for each side of the make-up bag in rainbow colours or others to your liking.
- Sew the two sides separately with the seam allowances facing out, using ½in (1.2cm) seam allowances.
- Cut two identical pieces 7⅜ x 11in (18.7 x 28cm) for the lining of the bag.
- Cut two pieces of 6⅜ x 10in (16.2 x 25.5cm) in batting.
- Sew on the zip and assemble the bag by folding the top of the bag onto its right side (corresponding to the seam allowance of ½in (1.2cm) and sew the zip on with a machine seam right at the edge.

- For the bag bottom cut two pieces 4 x 8½in (10 x 21.6cm), one in fabric and one in lining.
- Cut one piece of batting, 3 x 7½in (7.6 x 19cm).
- Quilt and sew the make-up bag as you did the larger bag.

- Make two loops out of a strip of 1½in (3.8cm) width. Fold the strip double, sew a seam along its length and cut it into two loops of 4in (10cm). Sew on a loop in each top corner.

Turquoise Treasure

This striking bag has a bright flannel inside and is covered in plastic on the outside.

- Cut out 12 squares each 6 x 6in (15.2 x 15.2cm) in turquoise and lime green fabrics.
- Sew the squares into two pieces, one for each side of the bag. Each piece is two squares high and three wide.
- Cut a 13 x 4in (33 x 10cm) rectangle; this will be for the bottom of the bag.
- Sew the pieces together with the bottom in the middle.
- Quilt and appliqué the bag in the same run, but first trace the flower motif (pattern on page 143) onto double-sided iron-on interfacing (see page 6) and iron 12 flowers onto the bag. Turquoise and lime green fabrics will look good.
- Quilt and appliqué the flowers freehand on the machine: place the lining, batting and patchwork on top of each other. Set your machine to a straight seam, attach the embroidery foot and lower the bottom feed dogs. Sew around each flower freehand two or three times, about ⅛in (2–3mm) inside the edge. The seams don't need to go exactly on top of each other.
- Cut up plastic to cover the bag completely and sew the plastic on the outside of the quilted and appliquéd bag along the edge of each square.
- Trim and follow the instructions for sewing a corner on page 65 and for binding on page 71.

- To make the handles, cut two strips of plastic 1¼ x 26½in (3.2 x 67.3cm).
- Cut two strips of 2½ x 27in (6.3 x 68.5cm) in the fabric you are using for the binding.
- Put a fabric strip and a plastic strip on top of each other, folding the fabric strip over and around the plastic.
- Sew a machine seam along the entire handle, so that the fabric is attached to the plastic.
- Do the same with the other handle and attach both handles to the bag with buttons.

Make-Up Bags

This is your chance to use some really bright fabrics to create little bags with big impact.

Easy Make-Up Bag

This is the easiest make-up bag in the book. You make it from a piece of brushed cotton, 8 x 12in (20.3 x 30.5cm). Quilt the piece with cotton batting and fabric for the lining. Then follow the procedures for a binding on page 71 and for making a fold in the side seam on page 66. The fold measures 1in (2.5cm). Add a zip (see page 73).

You can see another version of this make-up bag overleaf.

Bright Make-Up Bag

- Cut out 12 squares each 3 x 3in (7.6 x 7.6cm) in turquoise and lime green fabrics.
- Sew the squares into two pieces, each one two squares high and three wide.
- Cut a 2½ x 8in (6.3 x 20.3cm) rectangle for the bottom and sew it on in between the two patchwork pieces.
- Quilt the bag with cotton batting and a fabric for a lining. Straight machine seams should look nice.
- Trim, but no more than is absolutely necessary.
- Then follow instructions for sewing a fold into the side seam on page 66, a binding around the opening on page 71 and how to sew in a zip with your machine on page 73.

Pastel Make-Up Bag

- Cut out 12 squares measuring 3 x 3in (7.6 x 7.6cm) in pastel fabrics.
- Sew the squares into two pieces, each one two squares high and three squares wide.
- Cut a 2½ x 8in (6.3 x 20.3cm) rectangle for the bottom and sew it on in between the two patchwork pieces.
- Quilt the make-up bag with cotton batting and a fabric for the lining. Straight machine seams should look nice.
- Trim the batting to the size of the bag.
- Then follow instructions for sewing a fold into the side seam on page 66, adding a binding around the top edge on page 71 and how to sew in a zip with your machine on page 73.

Plastic Fantastic

This bag may seem a little strange. Not only is it round and pink, it is made out of a plastic tablecloth! If you feel like making one for yourself, here are the instructions.

- Sew bias binding around the top half of each bag part.
- Fold the third tablecloth circle double to make a pocket and put it on the outside of one bag part with the bottom edge to bottom edge.
- Sew it on with a seam down the middle of the bag, giving you two pockets.
- Join up the two parts of the bag with bias binding. Extend the binding a little over the bias binding you sewed on earlier.

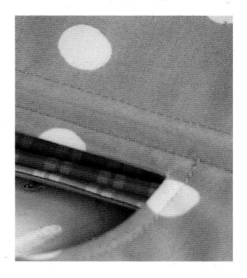

- Cut out three circles in a plastic tablecloth for the outside, two circles of cotton batting and two circles for lining, all with a diameter of 15in (38cm).
- Sew the handle opening first: trace a stencil for the handle opening onto paper and cut out.
- Put the stencil on the wrong side of one plastic circle, about 1in (2.5cm) from the edge, and trace around it with a pencil.
- Put one batting circle one lining circle (right side up) and one tablecloth circle (right side down) on top of each other.
- Stitch in the pencil line from the stencil for the handle opening.
- Cut out the handle opening

with a ¼in (7mm) seam and cut a few notches in the allowance where it curves.
- Turn the bag part the right way out by pushing the tablecloth through the new opening.
- Trim the opening.
- Sew two seams straight across both parts of the bag just below the handle opening with about ½in (1.2cm) between the two (see the photo above).
- Also stitch around the curved handle openings.
- Insert a wooden stick 7in (17.8cm) long between the seams that go across the bag, sealing it in with a seam at both ends.

Say It With Flowers

The flowers and leaves on this stunning bag are appliquéd on by hand but the bag itself is machine quilted.

- Cut out a piece of linen 12 x 22½in (30.5 x 57cm).
- Appliqué on flowers and leaves by hand, using freezer paper (see page 7): trace the motifs from page 143 onto the matt side of the paper and then cut out the motifs.
- Iron on the freezer paper with the waxed side facing the right side of the fabric.

- Cut out the motifs, each with ³⁄₁₆in (5mm) seam allowances.
- Tack each motif in position on the linen.
- Appliqué with little whipstitches from right to left (left to right if you are left-handed). Push in the seam allowance with your needle as you sew, while holding the seam allowance down with your left thumb (right thumb for the left-handed).
- Now it should be easy to tear the freezer paper off the motif.
- You can make the little blue berries by tacking around each circle, about ³⁄₁₆in (5mm) inside the raw edge. Pull the thread to make a small berry. Push in a tiny bit of batting to give your berry some volume before appliquéing it on the linen with tiny stitches.
- Cut out cotton batting and fabric for the inside and quilt it all together with straight, diagonal machine seams. Begin at the edge of the bag and stop at the motif. Begin sewing in the line near the motif and continue to the edge of the bag.
- Trim, and follow the instructions for sewing a corner on page 65 and a binding on page 71.
- You can close the bag by including a loop in the binding. Make the loop out of a fabric strip 1½ x 4½in (4 x 11.5cm) that is ironed double, wrong sides together. Then open it so that the long raw edges can be folded in towards the ironed edge. Fold it back into the first pressed edge. Stitch along the edge.
- Sew on a button on the opposite site of the bag.
- See page 70 to make the bag handles. These are 13in (33cm) long and ¾in (2cm) wide when finished. Follow the instructions for Handle A without batting.
- Fasten the handles by folding in ½in (1.2cm) and sewing them on the bag by machine. The distance between the handles is 2½in (6.3cm).
- To add a bottom plate refer to page 72.

Make-Up Bag

I have also made a little make-up bag to go with this bag. You will find the pattern on page 143.

Toilet Bags

follow the instructions to sew a corner on page 65, a binding around the top on page 71 and how to fit a zip by machine on page 73.

- I have appliquéd little hearts on the front of my bag. That was done after the rest of the bag was completed. The hearts have been appliquéd on by hand with little whipstitches reaching into the batting but not into the lining.
- I first made one circle of seven hearts, and then another seven hearts in an outside circle.

Heart Circle

- Cut out four rectangles of 5 x 6½in (12.7 x 16.5cm) in light pink fabrics.
- Sew them into one piece, two patches high and two wide.
- Cut a piece for the back of the bag, 9½ x 12½in (24 x 32cm). This should correspond to the joined-up rectangles.
- Cut a bottom piece 4½ x 8in (11.5 x 20.3cm) and sew it between the two sides pieces.
- Quilt the toilet bag with cotton batting and lining – straight machine seams will look good.
- Trim the batting to the size of the bag.
- I have appliquéd little hearts on the front of my bag. That was done after the bag was quilted. Eighteen hearts were placed inside a circle with a diameter of 6in (15.2cm). These hearts were appliquéd on using the machine. Use a straight stitch and move somewhat haphazardly across all the hearts.
- Now follow the instructions to sew a corner on page 65, a binding around the top on page 71 and how to fit a zip by machine on page 73.

These charming toilet bags are perfect for all your little essentials.

Red Hearts

- Cut out six squares each 5 x 5in (12.7 x 12.7cm) in light pink and green fabrics.
- Sew them into one piece, two patches high and four wide.
- Cut a piece for the back of the bag, 9½ x 14in (24 x 35.5cm). This should correspond to the joined-up squares.
- Cut a bottom piece 4½ x 9½in (11.5 x 24cm) and sew it on between the two side pieces.
- Quilt the bag with cotton batting and lining – straight machine seams will look good.
- Trim the batting to the size of the bag and then

Cosmetic Bags

Two make-up bags with different looks. One has many little squares, the other is in a striped fabric, but they have the same measurements and are made the same way, so you might as well make both while you are at it!

Candy

- Cut out 80 squares each measuring 1½ x 1½in (3.8 x 3.8cm) in strong pastel or candy-coloured fabrics.
- Sew them together into two pieces, five squares high and eight wide.
- Cut out a piece for the bottom, 3½ x 5in (9 x 12.7cm) and sew it on in the middle between the two side pieces.
- Quilt the make-up bag with cotton batting and lining. Straight machine seams will look good.
- Trim the batting to the size of the bag.
- Now follow the instructions to sew a corner on page 65, a binding around the top on page 71 and how to fit a zip by machine on page 73.

Striped Pink

Make this bag as for the Candy bag above, but use one piece of fabric instead of the little squares. To make the striped version you only need the measurements for the side pieces, which are 5 x 8½in (12.7 x 21.6cm). For the rest, follow the instructions above.

Zipped Pockets Bag

This bag is made out of two zipped pockets that have been sewed together and given a pair of ready-made handles.

- Cut out two pieces of linen, batting and lining, each 11 x 23in (28 x 58.4cm). This is for two pockets.
- Quilt one pocket freehand on the machine in a flower motif. The other one you might quilt in a grid pattern. That too can be done on the machine, but then you will be better off using the upper feed dogs.
- To complete your pockets follow the instructions on page 68 for making a pocket with zip. The zip can be placed about 3½in (8.9cm) from the edge/ fold of one pocket and 2½in (6.3cm) from the edge of the other pocket.
- Put the pockets together, back to back, with zips facing out. Sew them together with a seam a little inside the very edge, and not right up to the top.
- Attach handles on the inside of the bag, one on each pocket, using loops and buttons.
- Instructions for the loops are given on page 90 for the Little Roses Bag.

Perfect Purses

Here you can make several different versions out of the same pattern. These purses are very practical, and you can use them for your sewing things or a lipstick and mirror. Have a go with tiny patches, cut out some flowers for an appliqué or sew on some pretty buttons. Make your own version by assembling pieces of fabric until they cover the basic pattern. If you would rather follow a pattern, make one of the bags shown below.

Linen Purse with Flower

- Use two pieces of linen, each 5in (12.7cm) high by 6in (15.2cm) wide and appliqué on a flower and leaf (pattern on page 143).
- All the purse bottoms are 4½ x 2in (11.5 x 5cm), and all measurements include a seam allowance of ¼in (7mm). Stitch between the two side pieces.

Black Purse

- Use a piece of fabric 5½ x 4in (14 x 10cm) and add on strips until you cover the basic pattern. The strips can be cut straight or a little at an angle.

Brown Squares Purse

- Sew together little squares, 1½ x 1½in (3.8 x 3.8cm). For this basic pattern you will need six squares across and five up on either side.

Other Brown Purses

- Join up little squares for one side of the purse, with a single piece of fabric for the other side. This purse can be made a little lower, with four squares up and six across.

Green Silk Purse

- Sew together two pieces of fabric, 5½ x 4in (14 x 10cm) and include one or two triangles in the seam. Make the triangle(s) from 2 x 2in (5 x 5cm) squares folded diagonally twice.

Assembling Your Purse

- When the outside of the bag has been sewn, quilt it with cotton batting and lining.
- Cut out the basic pattern in freezer paper and iron it on the quilted piece. Then cut out the purse by following the edge of the pattern, which includes a seam allowance of ¼in (7mm). Tear off the freezer paper.
- Sew on bias binding at each opening. For bias binding cut a strip 1½in (3.8cm) wide and sew it on from the inside of the purse with a seam allowance of ¼in (7mm). You will achieve the best result by cutting the strip diagonally on the fabric.
- Fold in the seam allowance and fold the strip over onto the right side.
- Sew down the strip with a seam right at the edge. This can also be done the other way round, by sewing the strip on from the right side and folding it over to the inside. Sew the strip down by hand.
- Then follow instructions for sewing zips by hand on page 73 and sewing a corner on page 65. Sew on the zip first, then do the side seams.

Denim Bags

I haven't stopped making denim bags yet, and neither has Kari Anne Holt. She has been good enough to let me use some of her models for this book. The bag on page 81 and the bag in 'fray technique' (page 123) are both her designs. I will give you the pattern for my own bags, and then guidance regarding Kari Anne's models.

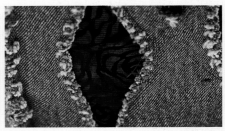

Frayed Denim Bags

- For each bag you will need to cut out:
  two denim pieces 9½ x 12in (24 x 30.5cm);
  two pieces for lining, 9½ x 12in (24 x 30.5cm);
  two pieces in a fabric that will form a backing for the denim and that will show as a decoration, 9½ x 12in (24 x 30.5cm);
  two pieces of cotton batting, 8½ x 11in (21.6 x 28cm).
- Put one piece of denim on one backing piece, right sides up, and sew seams either in a grid pattern or in curved, horizontal lines. Repeat with the other two pieces.
- Now put one decorated denim piece and one lining piece wrong sides together, with a piece of batting in between. The batting should be in the middle, with the fabric extending the same amount on all sides.
- Pin together all three layers – denim, batting and lining – and machine quilt in, or close to, the lines you have sewed already.
- Cut out the denim along the quilt seams so that the fabric

underneath shows. Cut around ¼in (7mm) from the seams.
- For the rest of the bag cut out:
  two side pieces in denim, 4 x 9½in (10 x 24cm);
  two side pieces in lining fabric, 4 x 9½in (10 x 24cm);
  two side pieces in batting, 3 x 8½in (7.6 x 21.6cm);
  one bottom in denim, 4 x 12in (10 x 30.5cm);
  one bottom in cotton batting, 3 x 11in (7.6 x 28cm).
- Put one denim piece and one piece of lining with wrong sides together with the batting in between. The batting should be in the middle, with the fabric extending the same amount on all sides.
- Repeat with the other pieces so that you get two side pieces and one bottom piece.
- Sew the bag together with ½in (1.2cm) seam allowances that face out.
- Sew a seam round the opening, ½in (1.2cm) in from the edge.
- When your bag is complete, cut a notch every ½in (1.2cm) in all seam allowances.
- Machine-wash the bag at 40 degrees centigrade and give it a go in the tumble dryer as well if you have one.

To make the handles

- On the bag with the rectangles (shown near left) you can sew on the handles by following the instructions for Handle A on page 70. The handles are 1in (2.5cm) wide and 27in (68.5cm) long when finished. Using a machine seam fasten them to the inside of the bag, and decorate with a lovely button if you like.
- For the bag with wavy lines (shown far right) I used ready-made bamboo handles that have been attached to the bag with the belt loops from a pair of jeans.

I made a pocket out of a jeans pocket by folding the jeans pocket double and including it in one of the side seams (shown below).

Kari Anne's Bag

Kari Anne's bag is so lovely! It has a bright red check lining and closes with a zip.

- This front and back are sewn in the same way as my bags on the previous page and you will need: two pieces of denim, 9 x 11in (23 x 28cm); two pieces of red check fabric, 9 x 11in (23 x 28cm); two pieces of batting, 8 x 10in (20.3 x 25.5cm).
- The side pieces and the bottom are sewn in the same way as my bags and you will need: two pieces of denim, 5 x 9in (12.7 x 23cm) for the sides; two pieces of red check fabric, 5 x 9in (12.7 x 23cm) for lining for the sides; two pieces of batting, 4 x 8in (10 x 20.3cm) for the sides; one piece of denim 5 x 11in (12.7 x 28cm) for the bottom; one piece of red check fabric 5 x 11in (12.7 x 28cm) for the bottom lining; one piece of batting 4 x 10in (10 x 25.5cm) for the bottom.
- If you want the same closing as Kari Anne, cut up two pieces of check fabric measuring 4 x 11in (10 x 28cm) and hem in both the short sides and one long side on each.
- Sew on an 11in (28cm) long zip, leaving the end of the zip a little outside the fabric. Include the two other long sides (that have no hem) with the seam around the opening.

Sewing Roll

If you are planning a sewing trip with your flowery bag, it might be nice to have somewhere to keep various sewing bits. This one is very easy to make, just have a go!

- Start by cutting out two pieces of linen, each 6 x 12in (15.2 x 30.5cm). One is the backing piece for the pockets, the other for the outside of the sewing roll.
- Cut out two pockets in linen, each 6 x 5in (15.2 x 12.7cm) and one pocket in linen, 6in (15.2cm) wide by 4in (10cm) high.
- A motif may be appliquéd on the bottom pocket (see page 110) and also, if you like, you can add a small label at the top of the backing piece. This label will make a nice pincushion.
- First hem the top of each pocket and sew the pocket on the back piece. The top pocket is the smallest, and it should be sewed on the back piece 6in (15.2cm) from the top of the sewing roll. The next pocket should be positioned 9in (23cm) from the top, and the last one should be left loose, as it will be included in the binding.
- Sew a binding around the entire sewing roll. Make a long loop out of a fabric strip that is 27in (68.5cm) long and 1½in (3.8cm) wide. Iron the strip wrong sides together, open it and fold the long sides in towards the first pressed edge. Fold back into the first press edge. Stitch along the edge. Fold the loop in two and fasten it to the sewing roll with a button.

Suppliers

UK

Coats Crafts UK
PO Box 22, Lingfield House, McMullen Road,
   Darlington, County Durham DL1 1YQ
tel: 01325 394200 (consumer helpline)
www.coatscrafts.co.uk
For Anchor stranded cotton (floss) and other
   embroidery supplies.

The Cotton Patch
1285 Stratford Road, Hall Green, Birmingham
   B28 9AJ
tel: 0121 702 2840
www.cottonpatch.co.uk
For patchwork and quilting supplies

Creative Grids
Unit 28 Swannington Road, Cottage Lane Industrial
   Estate, Broughton Astley, Leicester LE9 6TU
tel: 0845 450 7722 or 0845 450 7733
tel international: 00 44 1455 285931 or 00 44 1455
   286787
www.creativegrids.com
For patchwork and quilting supplies, including
   quilters' rulers

DMC Creative World
Pullman Road, Wigston, Leicestershire LE18 2DY
tel: 0116 281 1040
fax: 0116 281 3592
www.dmc/cw.com
For stranded cotton (floss) and other embroidery
   supplies

Madeira Threads (UK) Ltd
PO Box 6, Thirsk, North Yorkshire YO7 3YX
tel: 01845 524880
email: info@madeira.co.uk
www.madeira.co.uk
For Madeira stranded cotton (floss) and other
   embroidery supplies

USA

The City Quilter
157 West 24th Street, New York, NY 1011
tel: 212 807 0390
For patchwork and quilting supplies (shop and mail
   order)

Connecting Threads
13118 NE 4th Street, Vancouver, WA 98684
tel: 1 800 574 6454
Email: customerservice@connectingthreads.com
www.connectingthreads.com
For general needlework and quilting supplies

eQuilter.com
5455 Spine Road, Suite E; Boulder, CO 80301
tel: USA Toll Free: 877-FABRIC-3 or: 303-527-0856
email: service@equilter.com
www.eQuilter.com
For patchwork fabrics

Joann Stores, Inc
5555 Darrow Road, Hudson Ohio
tel: 1 888 739 4120
email: guest service@jo-annstores.com
www.joann.com
For general needlework and quilting supplies (mail
   order and shops across the US)

M & J Buttons
1000 Sixth Avenue, New York, NY 10018
tel: 212 391 6200
www.mjtrim.com
For beads, buttons, ribbons and trimmings

The WARM Company
954 East Union Street, Seattle WA 98122
tel: 1 800 234 WARM
www.warmcompany.com
UK Distributor: W. Williams & Sons Ltd
tel: 017 263 7311
For polyester filling, cotton wadding (batting) and
   Steam-a-Seam fusible web

Patterns

All templates are 100% unless otherwise stated.

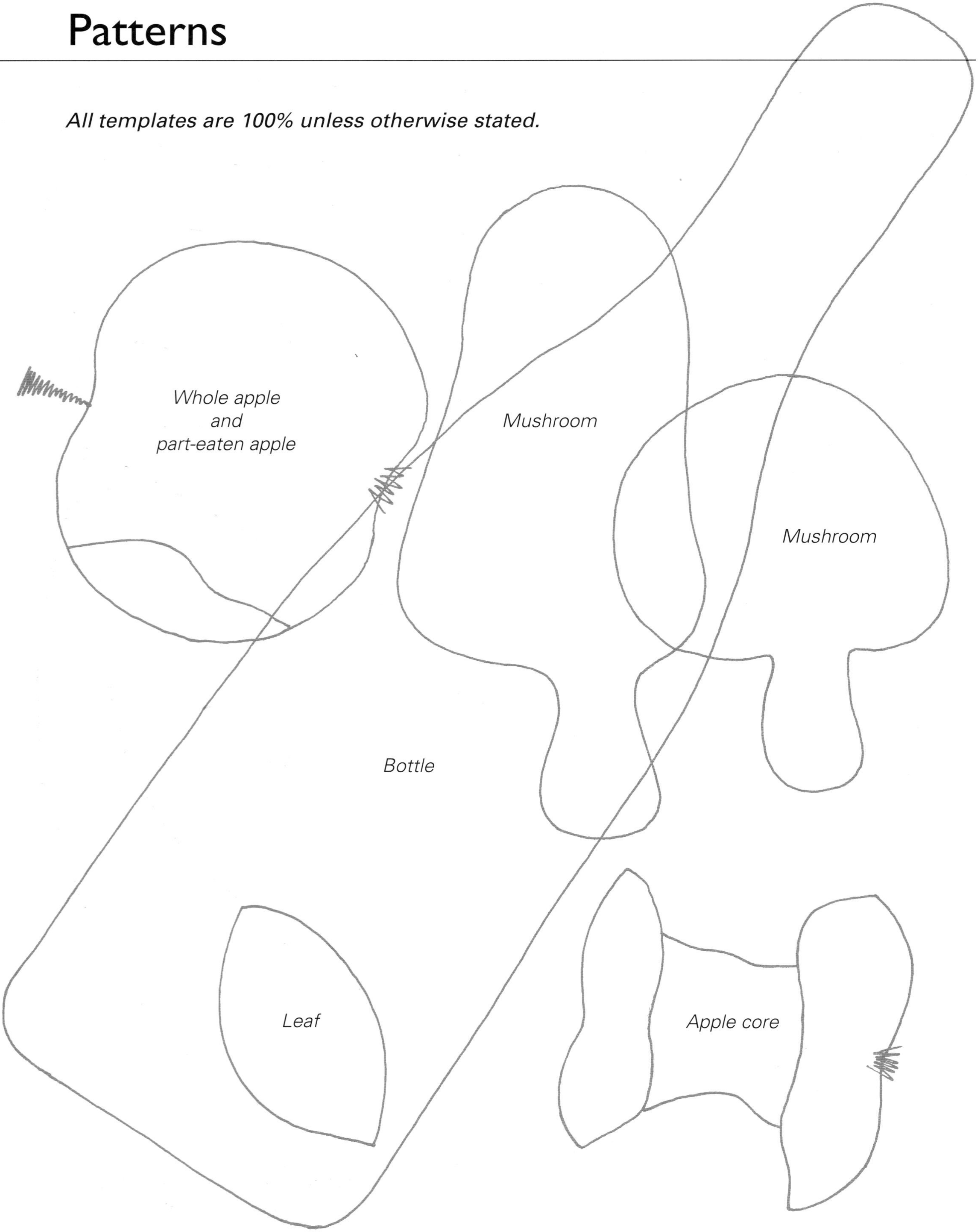

Whole apple
and
part-eaten apple

Mushroom

Mushroom

Bottle

Leaf

Apple core

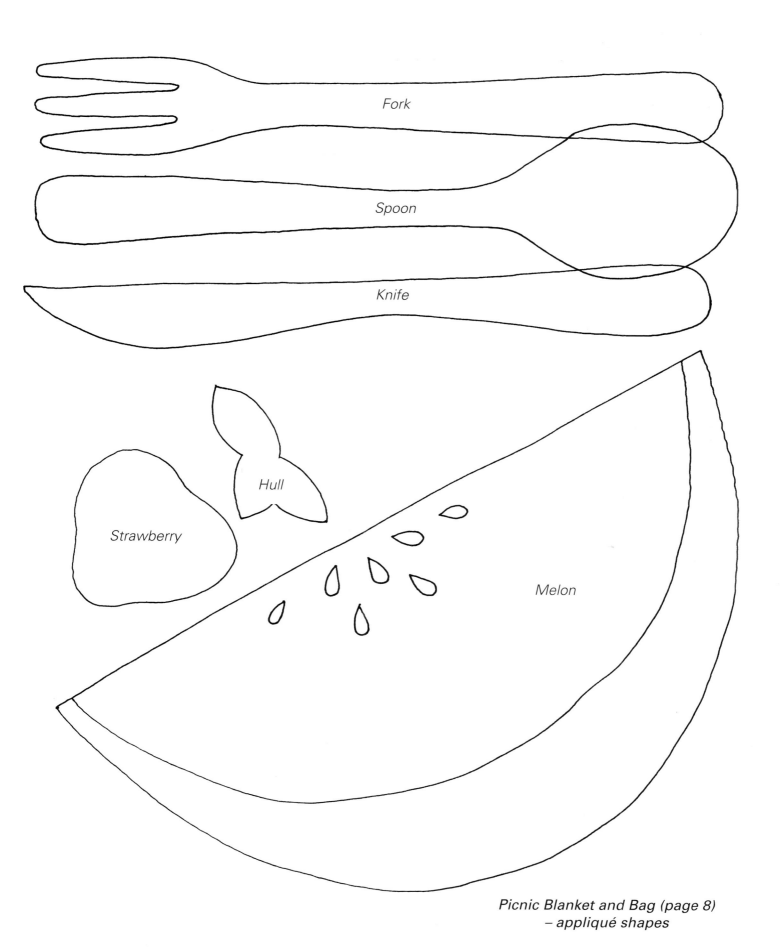

Fork

Spoon

Knife

Hull

Strawberry

Melon

Picnic Blanket and Bag (page 8)
– appliqué shapes

Summer Flowers (page 18) –
appliqué shapes

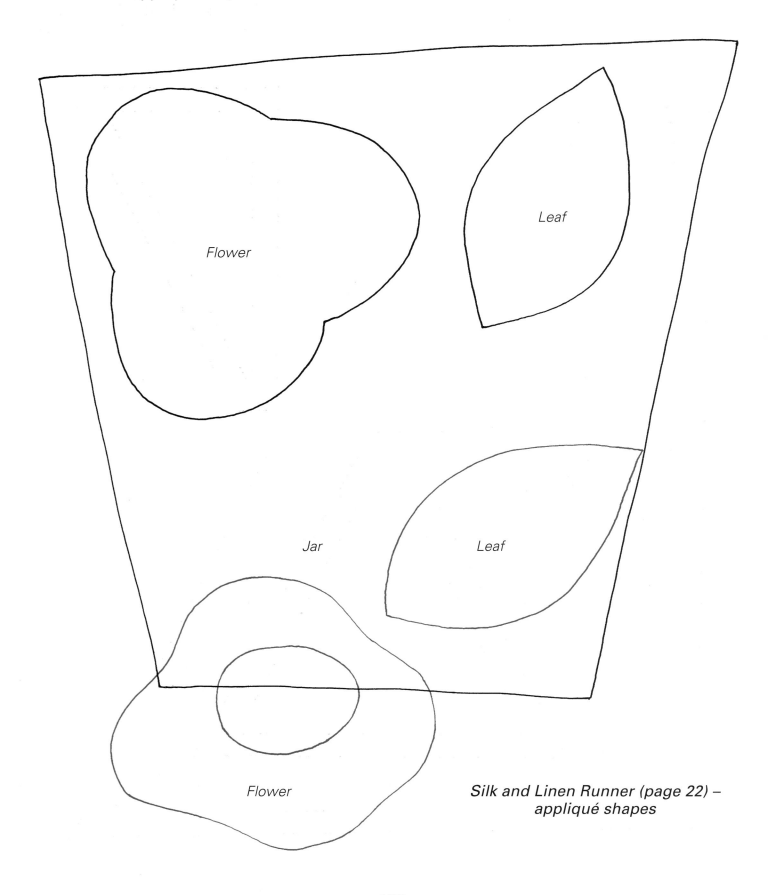

Flower

Leaf

Jar

Leaf

Flower

Silk and Linen Runner (page 22) –
appliqué shapes

6
Rich Coffee Quilt (page 16),
Linen Tablecloth (page 20)

4
Rhapsody in Blue (page 12),
Jungle Rumble (page 14)

3
Flora Quilt (page 24),
Guinea Hens (page 29),
Flowers Wall Hanging (page 18),
You Are My Sunshine (page 30)

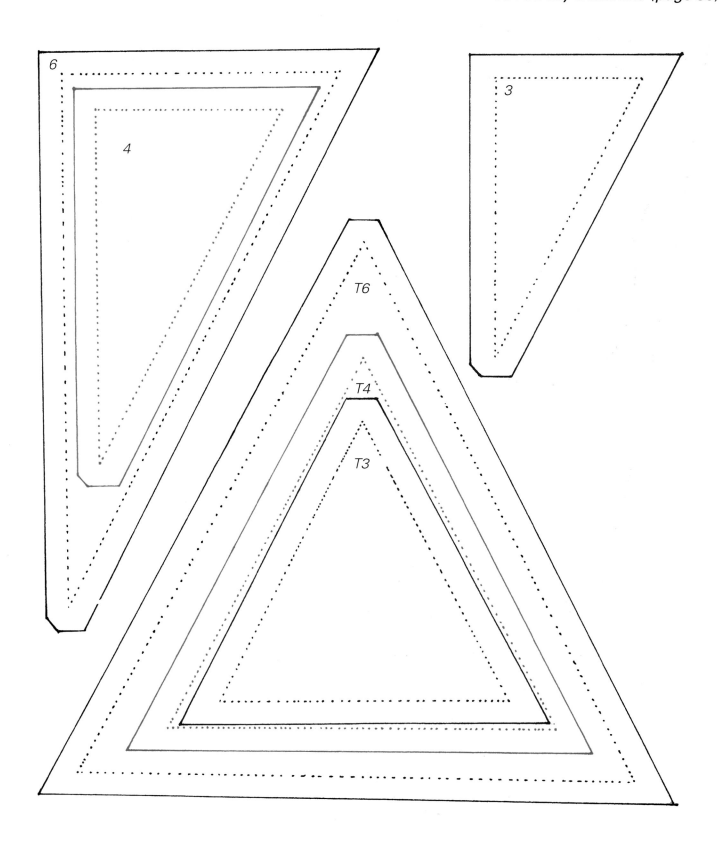

6

4

3

T6

T4

T3

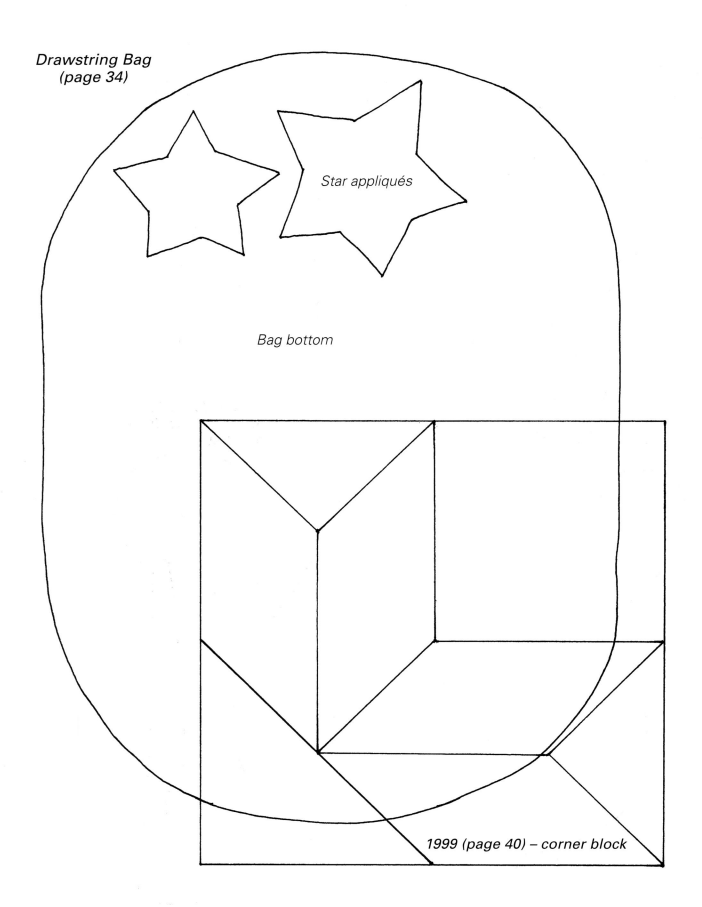

Drawstring Bag
(page 34)

Star appliqués

Bag bottom

1999 (page 40) – corner block

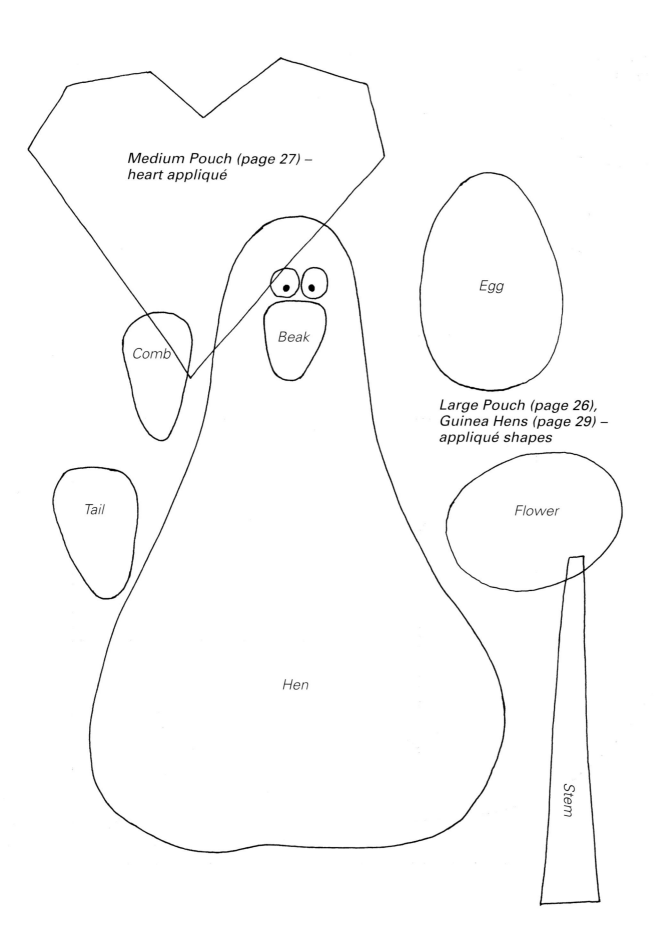

Medium Pouch (page 27) – heart appliqué

Egg

Comb

Beak

Large Pouch (page 26), Guinea Hens (page 29) – appliqué shapes

Flower

Tail

Hen

Stem

131

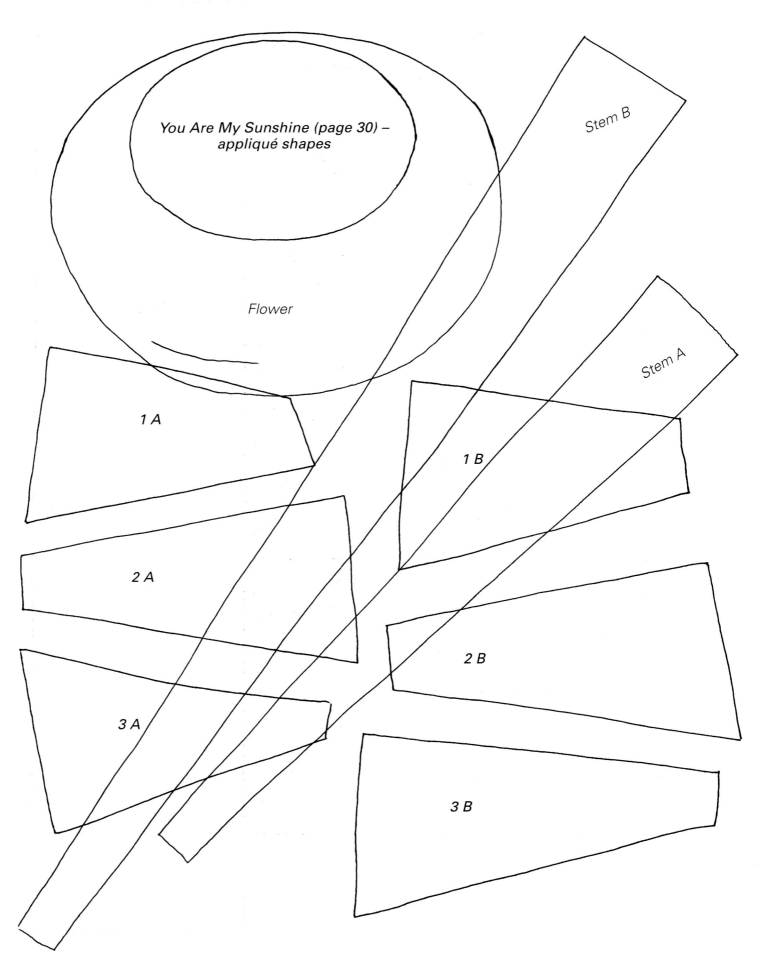

*You Are My Sunshine (page 30) –
appliqué shapes*

Flower

Stem B

Stem A

1 A

1 B

2 A

2 B

3 A

3 B

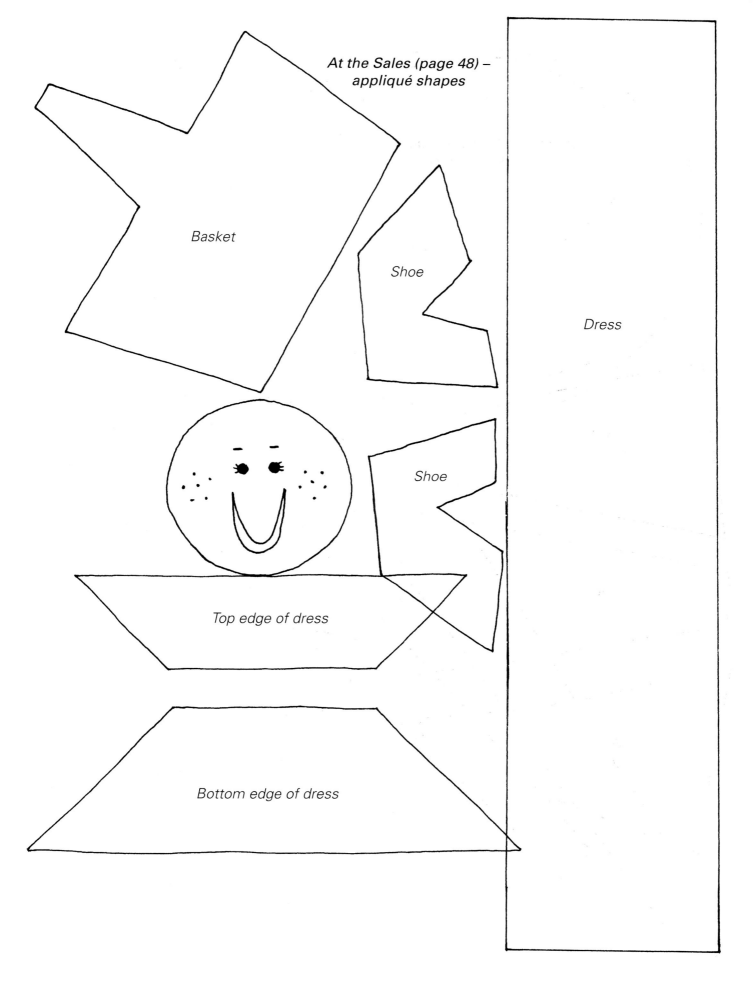

At the Sales (page 48) –
appliqué shapes

Basket

Shoe

Dress

Shoe

Top edge of dress

Bottom edge of dress

At the Sales (page 48) –
appliqué shapes

At the Sales (page 48) –
appliqué shapes

At the Sales (page 48) –
appliqué shapes

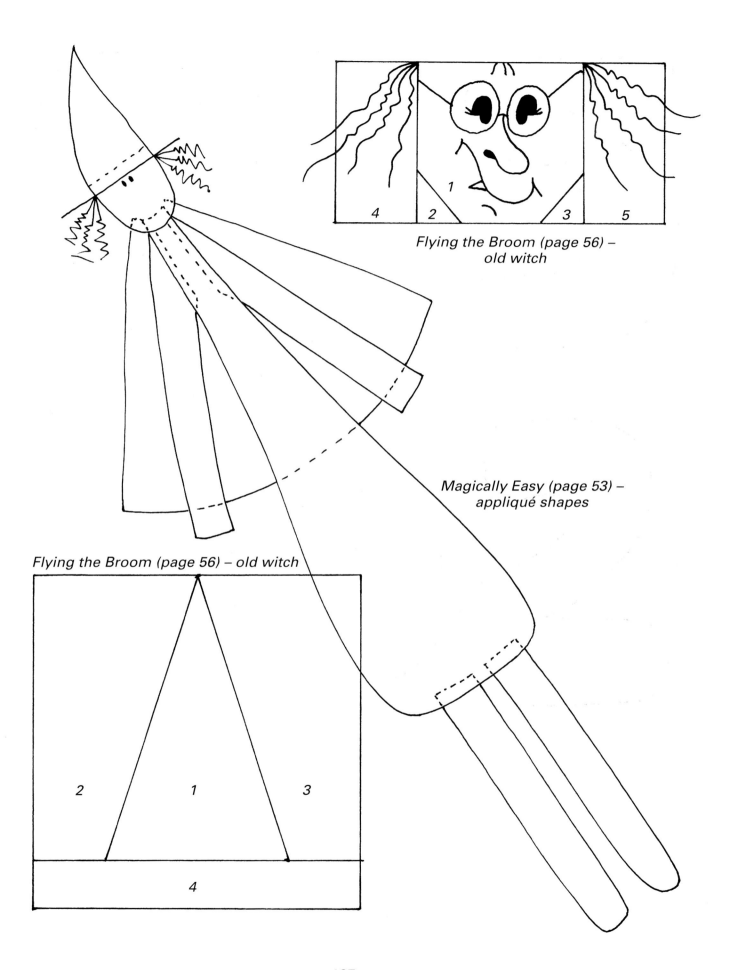

Flying the Broom (page 56) – old witch

4 | 2 | 1 | 3 | 5

Magically Easy (page 53) – appliqué shapes

Flying the Broom (page 56) – old witch

2 | 1 | 3

4

Templates on this page will need enlarging by 200% on a photocopier

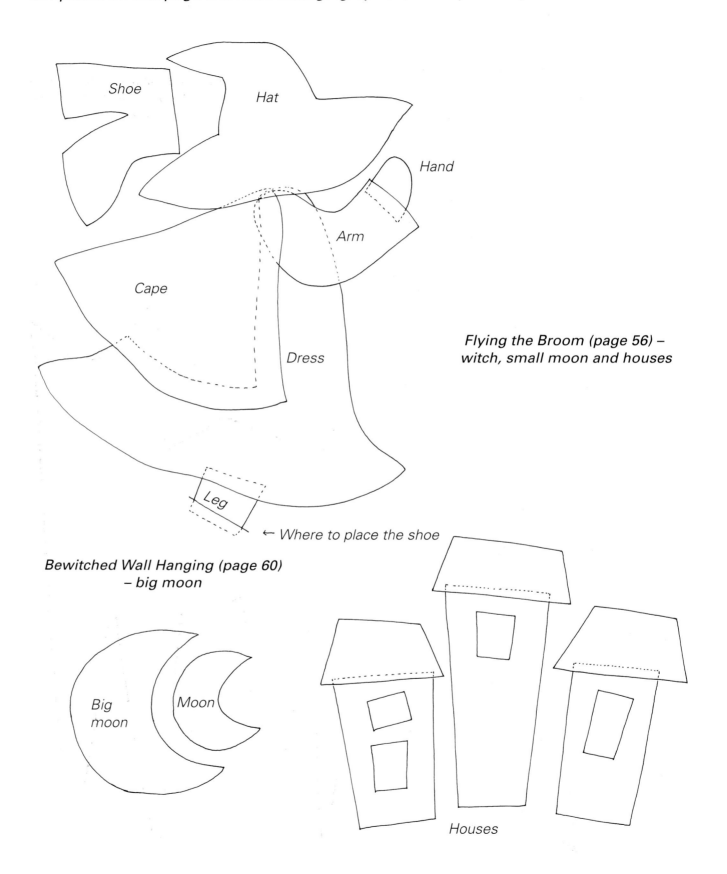

Shoe

Hat

Hand

Arm

Cape

Dress

Flying the Broom (page 56) – witch, small moon and houses

Leg

← Where to place the shoe

Bewitched Wall Hanging (page 60) – big moon

Big moon

Moon

Houses

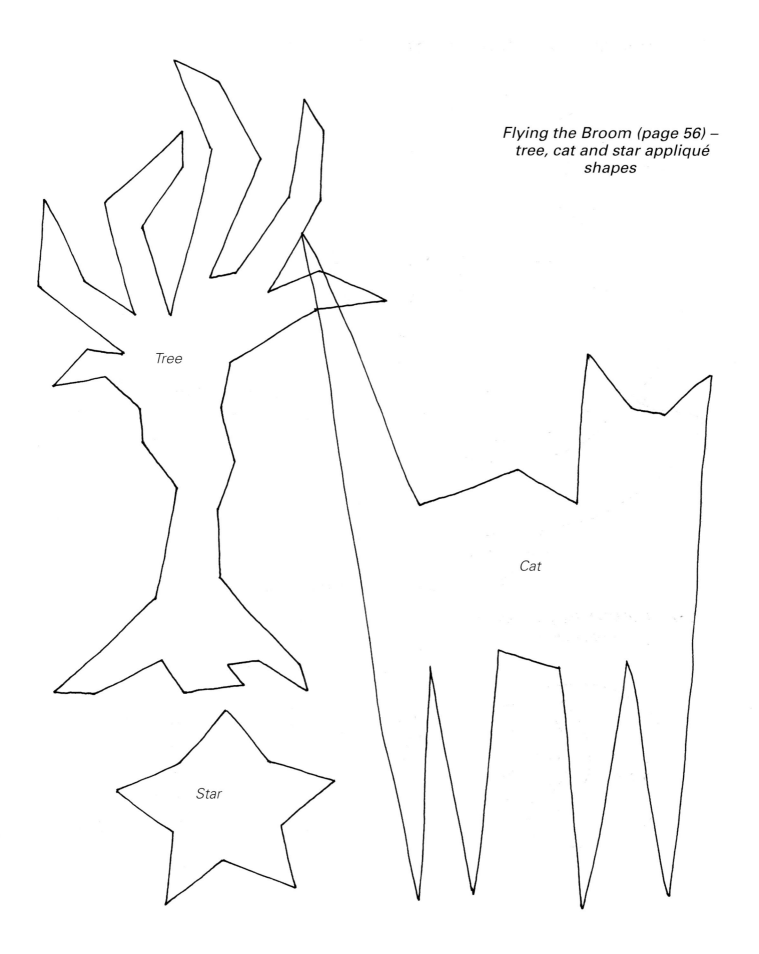

Flying the Broom (page 56) – tree, cat and star appliqué shapes

Tree

Cat

Star

Round-Handled Bags (page 92) – making roses

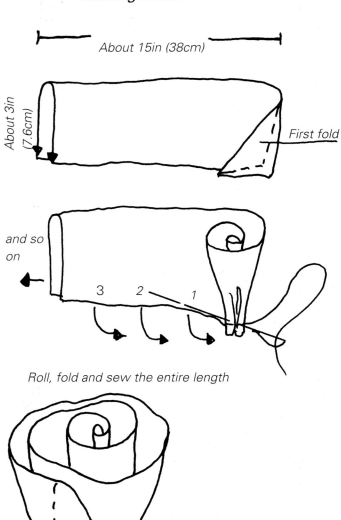

About 15in (38cm)

About 3in (7.6cm)

First fold

and so on

3   2   1

Roll, fold and sew the entire length

Tuck in the end

Round-Handled Bags (page 92) – making leaves

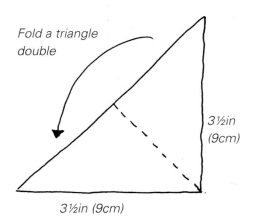

Fold a triangle double

3½in (9cm)

3½in (9cm)

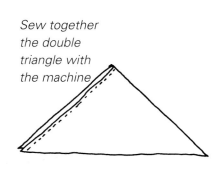

Sew together the double triangle with the machine

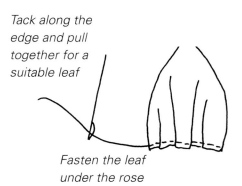

Tack along the edge and pull together for a suitable leaf

Fasten the leaf under the rose

Two in One (page 100) – making a yo-yo

- Cut out the circle in fabric
- Fold in about ³/₁₆ in (5mm) seam allowance around the entire circle while sewing little tacking stitches along the edge.
- Pull the thread and gather the circle together into a yo-yo.
- Fasten the thread with a couple of backstitches.
- Fasten the opening with a few little cross stitches through all the layers. Try to get the opening as near the centre as possible.

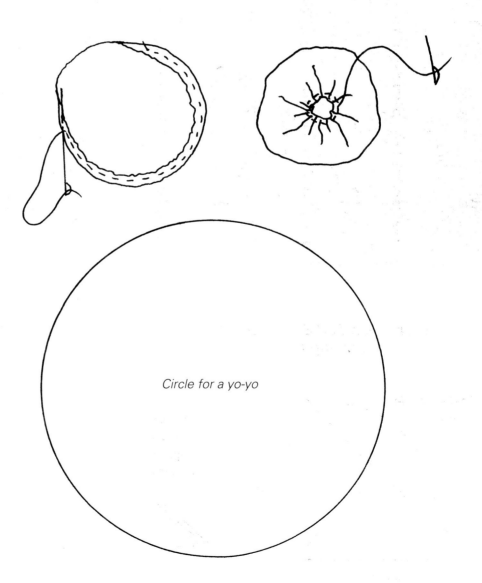

Circle for a yo-yo

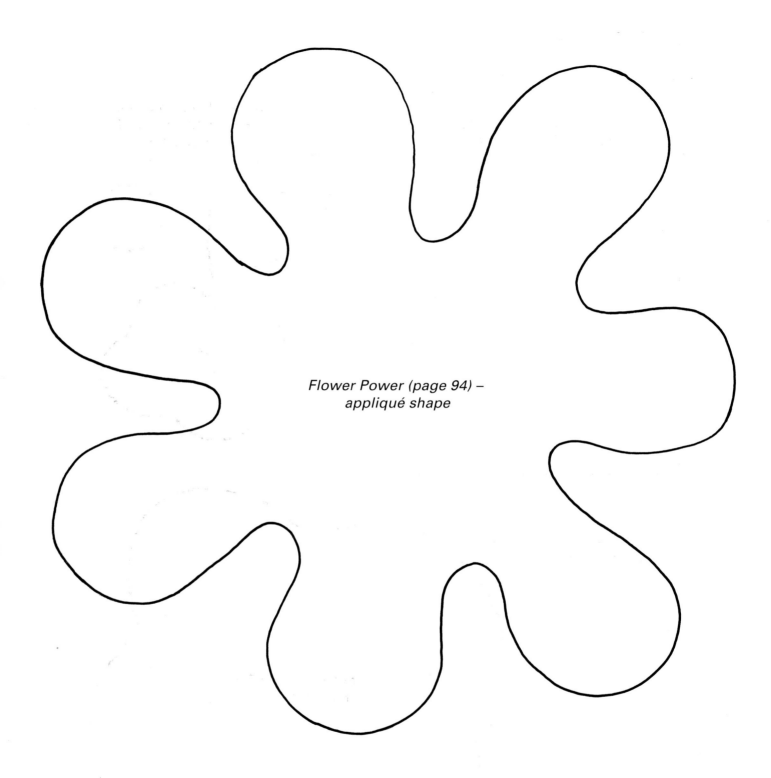

Flower Power (page 94) –
appliqué shape

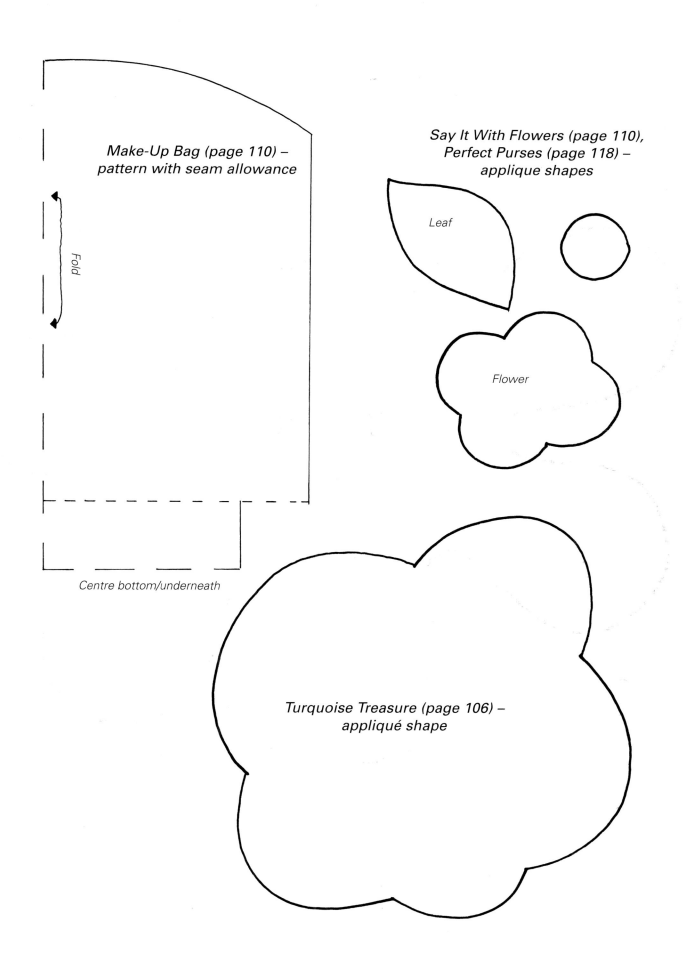

Make-Up Bag (page 110) –
pattern with seam allowance

Fold

Centre bottom/underneath

Say It With Flowers (page 110),
Perfect Purses (page 118) –
applique shapes

Leaf

Flower

Turquoise Treasure (page 106) –
appliqué shape

Index